MW00395909

Lonely ☮ planet

The
JOY
of
Birdwatching

Contents

Africa & the Middle East

Americas & Antarctica

© Steffen Foerster / Shutterstock; Jonathan Gregson / Lonely Planet; Philip Lee Harvey / Lonely Planet;

Introduction

Joy comes in all shapes and sizes, and if birding is something that flutters your feathers, the source of that giddy elation could be something as small as a tiny hummingbird or English wren, or as enormous as an ostrich, cassowary or rhea. It could be something as simple as swifts swooping through summer skies, or something as edge-of-the-envelope as tramping through the rainforest to observe the flamboyant display of Ecuador's cock of the rock or Indonesia's red bird of paradise.

Exploring the world's most rewarding bird encounters was the inspiration for the creation of this book, which looks at birding experiences high and low, hot and cold, dry and humid, remote and urban, from all over the planet. Inside, you'll find 180 amazing close encounters with birdlife – some close to home, some on the opposite side of the globe, but all with the same glorious potential to inspire joy.

Many people plan trips specifically around birdwatching, but our ambition for this book is to get you thinking more broadly about how nature can be worked into your own travel itineraries. A trip doesn't have to be to a famous birding reserve with an expert guide to deliver a world-class bird encounter. Indeed, with a keen eye, birdwatching experiences can materialise in the most prosaic of settings, from suburban lanes in Cape Coral, Florida to the banks of the River Thames in London.

This book is not intended to be a dry treatise on the science of birds – plenty of books do that job perfectly well already! Our aim in *The Joy of Birdwatching* is to bring you along on the experience of meeting some of the world's most remarkable birds, guided by writers who get the same sense of unbridled, uninhibited joy from encounters with birds big and small.

While all the experiences we explore are backed up by practical advice and suggestions of similar birding hot-spots to explore, the focus is on the pleasure of the experience: the sights, the sounds the sensations, the settings, and above all the emotions that seeing birds can inspire. If witnessing penguins in Antarctica, or parrots in Peru, or the dances of red-crowned cranes in Japan has ever been on your travel bucket list, let this book set you on the path to finding that joy.

How to use this book

This book presents 60 memorable birdwatching experiences from all over the world, organised by region, each accompanied by two more suggestions of other great bird encounters that are similar or nearby. These pieces explore both the joy of birding and the practicalities – what makes these birds, locations and encounters so special, what are the rewards and challenges, and the 'don't miss' aspects of each experience. Feature profiles provide at-a-glance reasons to go, plus the optimal month or months to visit. In the Q&A panel, you can read insights and thoughts from birding experts closely associated with that location. Alternatively, the My Birding Joy panel gives a personal account of the delight experienced by the writer of the piece. To help you start planning your trip, each entry has a factbox detailing how to get there, how accessible the site is, and the best times to come. Check the index to find birding experiences listed by country and type..

By Joe Bindloss

© Erni / Shutterstock

Foreword

By Tenijah Hamilton

One of the great tragedies of growing up is that no one asks you what your favourite dinosaur is anymore. It's a nearly imperceptible shift, but one day, your whole life revolves around syllables too big for your mouth to handle, and the next day, no one has time to hear about your near-encyclopaedic knowledge of the Stegosaurus.

For me, becoming a birder in the summer of 2020 – against a backdrop of societal upheaval in every direction – reacquainted me with the idea of joy for joy's sake. Reckless joy. Silly joy. Unbridled joy. Joy that made me feel very small again in an enormous world. Joy for the joy of it, that couldn't be measured by a KPI or assessed at a performance review.

For many of us, the pursuit of curiosity for curiosity's sake gets supplanted by the need for grown-up things like laptops and alarm clocks that screech the most contrived sounds ever put together. Priorities become refocused on the things we need to do to make money or be respected or maintain status. To varying degrees, these things can and do make us happy, but it's easy to forget to leave space for the cultivation of simple joy.

Since I started birding, I've discovered that joy can look like a fuzzy flying tennis ball zooming past your window, until you realize it's a goldfinch. It can sound like an owl outside your window every morning, when in reality, it's a mourning dove. It can be the smell of flowers in springtime, blooming for pollinators that form a favourite buffet for our bird friends.

Birdwatching is a bit of a misnomer, because engaging with birds requires the mindful engagement of all of your senses. For me, a big part of the joy comes from the act of wandering and wondering (or the Double-Dubs as I like to call it).

One of my favourite things about the birding community is the way it makes space for every kind of birder, at every level of ability. Not every person who goes birding can see or hear the birds. Not everyone on a birding walk will be able to walk. Not every birder is a seasoned expert. Part of the beauty of birding is the fact that it is accessible to almost every type of person.

© Ellen McKnight / Alamy Stock Photo

I've trudged through marshland wildlife refuges with octogenarians on motorized wheelchairs, assessing trails for their suitability for people with mobility needs. I've listened to teens waxing lyrical about the house-building plans of purple martins. I've schlepped through unseasonable frost in the Pacific Northwest to speak to people incarcerated in the prison system who still find ways to bird. And I've birded with kids of all ages, with insatiable appetites for questioning the 'why' of things.

As a kid, you notice everything. Every touch, smell, taste, sound and sensation you encounter is hungrily absorbed, indelibly imprinting on your mind the act of living. To me, birding feels like a mindful re-engagement of that process. As a birder, everything you feel, hear, smell and see is also imprinting on you, making you a stronger birder and a better steward of the great outdoors.

The best birders I know treat bird watching like a chilled-out game of Detective. Finding and identifying birds involves the fastidious study of evidence: a certain berry on a bush, earthworms

"There is a sense of liberation about becoming a novice at something"

surfacing to do a dewy sun salutation, the construction materials of various nests.

Birding is always a learning experience. In a flash of feathers, you might mistake a house finch for a towhee, but it's all part of the process of honing your identification skills. And how often, as adults, do we allow ourselves the luxury of being wrong? There's something liberating about becoming a novice at something – relearning the important truth that experience can be as important as excellence and not every hobby has to be a side hustle.

For years now, I've called myself a bird girl in training. Despite being the proud owner of my own pair of 'bins' and hosting and producing

© Michael G Mckinne / Shutterstock; Tasnia Maleki

four seasons of a podcast about the social, environmental and moral imperative to save birds, I'm reticent to give up the title.

I think it's because being a bird girl in training makes me feel like I am still growing in my birding journey. It means I can give myself permission to squeal when I see a bird that looks like a cartoon brought to life (yes, I'm looking at you, Australian noisy miner) or giggle every time someone calls a yellow-rumped warbler a 'butter butt'. That's the thing about joy – it should be childlike, nonsensical and fervent, and you should be relentless in pursuing it.

Before I knew anything about flocks and feathers, I was a public-school-attending, metro-card-toting, concrete-jungle-dwelling kid from Brooklyn – an unlikely candidate to end up writing the foreword for this particular book, perhaps! But if I had known that the birding community was as expansive as I now know it to be, I would have been able to tap into this particular joy much earlier on in life.

It's gratifying to know there is now a Black Birders' Week, and that the Feminist Bird Club has chapters nationwide, and that people from all walks of life gather at the parks in neighbouring boroughs to gawk at handsome ducks every weekend.

I hope that reading the stories in this book will help you to tap into that feeling of joy from when you were a kid. You have full permission to stop thinking about tax codes and wine pairings and shoes that provide the adequate level of arch support, and instead consider the question: What is your favourite dinosaur, and why is it a bird?

Tenijah Hamilton hosts and produces a podcast called *Bring Birds Back* for BirdNote. She is also the Chief Community Officer for Hopebound, an Atlanta-based organization providing therapy for under-resourced youth.

Previous spread: Birds bathe in the fountain in Central Park's Secret Garden in New York, USA

Far left: A yellow-rumped warbler

Left: Tenijah Hamilton, watching birds in Atlanta, USA

© Jonathan Gregson / Lonely Planet

Africa & the Middle East

Paddle in toe-numbing surf with African penguins

 Endemic species, landscapes, views

 Year-round

SOUTH AFRICA

It's a sight guaranteed to make you smile: a beach covered with waddling, hopping and scurrying African penguins. Welcome to Boulders, home to the largest mainland penguin colony of penguins in South Africa. From Cape Town, it's the most convenient and best-set-up place to observe these charming black-and-white flightless birds up close and in the wild.

Named after the giant, 540-million-year-old hunks of granite dividing this series of compact, sandy coves, Boulders would be a spectacular location even without the presence of the penguins. Endemic Cape Floral Kingdom plant life flourishes on the hills on the one side, while the clear waters of False Bay sparkle on the other. Just up the road is the historic naval base of Simon's Town, while further south are the even more spectacular vistas of Cape Point.

Boulders is a protected area within Table Mountain National Park, so you'll pay the park's entry fee at the Visitor Centre near Seaforth Sq, from where two boardwalks run to Foxy Beach. The sand here is off limits to the public, but there are two viewing platforms where you can watch the action. Like nonchalant, stunted supermodels, the dapper penguins blithely ignore the armies of camera-toting tourists snapping away at their antics.

Admire – but from a distance
A third boardwalk, Willis Walk, starts just outside the Visitor Centre and runs north to Boulders Beach. Along the way you may encounter penguins sunbathing on the rocks; the more adventurous birds shimmy up to linger beside the boardwalk itself.

Right: The African penguin has distinctive pink patches of skin above its eyes

Below: Boulders Beach, near Cape Town, is a popular place to see the penguins

© Pcala / Shutterstock; Sergey Uryadnikov / Shutterstock; Jesus Cobaleda / Shutterstock

Q&A

What's the big appeal of penguins?
They are extremely endearing as they go about their 'gnome-like' ways. Think of the movie *Happy Feet*. I also enjoy watching bonded pairs preening one another for extended periods between bouts of 'braying' to further reinforce the pair's bond.

Why are there scruffy looking penguins in December and January?
That's when penguins undertake a complete moult, lasting up to two weeks. They remain ashore and look extremely dishevelled.

Is the colony at Boulders sustainable?
Over the past few years, we have seen a noticeable contraction in the number of African penguins breeding in the Boulders area. We have serious personal doubts as to whether the breeding population at Boulders will exist beyond 2030.

Patrick Cardwell,
Avian Leisure Birding & Wildlife Safaris cofounder

Left: Returning from hunting fish and squid

Right: New Zealand's crested penguins nest among tree roots and rocks around the south coast

Don't Miss

→ **Paddling in the water with the penguins**

→ **Watching penguins sunbathing on the beach**

→ **Taking in spectacular sea views at nearby Cape of Good Hope**

At Boulders it is permitted to walk on the sand and mingle with the waddling penguins. If your skin is thick enough to withstand False Bay's frigid waters (even at the height of summer the average temperature is 20°C/68°F), go for a paddle or a swim beside these charming aquatic birds. But don't get too close or attempt to feed the penguins. They may look cute and cuddly, but their beaks are as sharp as razors, and they have no qualms about nipping an offending finger or nose if they feel threatened.

Penguins in Africa

One of the world's 18 penguin species, African penguins were once called jackass penguins on account of their donkey-like braying. They are monogamous, with lifelong partners taking turns to incubate their eggs and feed their young. From just two breeding pairs, thought to have migrated from Dyer Island in 1982, the Boulders colony has grown to about 2200 in recent years.

However, African penguins are now a critically endangered species, their total population having been depleted by some 90% from an estimated 1.5 million in the early 20th century. Today, the penguins face multiple threats, including predation from seals, climate change and widespread pollution along the shorelines. Under such circumstances, seeing them en masse at Boulders feels like a privilege to be treasured.

Find Your Joy

Getting there
Fly into Cape Town International Airport, where you can hire a car to drive the 29 miles (47km) southwest to Boulders. Cape Town travel agencies can also organise transfers and guided tours to Boulders. Alternatively, if you're staying in nearby Simon's Town, you can get to the reserve on foot: it's a 2-mile (3km) walk.

Accessibility
One of the boardwalks from the Boulders Visitor Centre to Foxy Beach is wheelchair accessible.

When to go
Peak breeding season is March to May. Hit the beach in the late afternoon when the penguins return to their nests after fishing during the day.

Further information
• Admission charge.
• Open year-round.
• No specialist facilities.
• Cafes and a restaurant next to the Boulders Visitor Centre.
• Accommodation in nearby Simon's Town.
• www.sanparks.org

Other Places to Peek at Penguins

Lake Moeraki, New Zealand

With a population estimated at 3000 pairs, Fiordland crested penguins are considered endangered. They can only be seen in the South Island's southwest corner, most easily along the shore of Lake Moeraki via guided tours from the Wilderness Lodge here. Known in Maori as tawaki, these cute characters are easily identified by the yellow feathered crests on their heads.

Don't miss

Admiring the striking plumage and honking squawks of these distinctive penguins.

Penneshaw Penguin Centre, Australia

The gateway to South Australia's Kangaroo Island, Penneshaw is a charming small town that's also the site of a colony of little penguins. These 13in-tall (33cm) birds – also known as fairy penguins – are the smallest of the world's penguins, sporting blue and white feathers that provide excellent camouflage against predators.

Don't miss

Joining a torchlit evening walk, organised by the Penguin Centre, to look for Penneshaw's 15 breeding pairs.

Embrace the dawn chorus in the Serengeti

 Stillness, sense of space, sunrise

 Year-round

TANZANIA

It's usually Serengeti's larger wildlife that gets the attention, and with roaming elephants, lions posing regally atop the kopjes (boulders), massive herds of migrating wildebeest and more, it's easy to see why. Yet, with over 500 bird species, Tanzania's most famous wildlife park is also one of East Africa's greatest birding areas.

Alive with birds

Stop for a moment anywhere in the park and you'll soon realise that the Serengeti is alive with birds. Weavers flit among the grasses. Sunbirds brighten the savannahs. An ostrich strides off into the distance. Guinea fowl chatter in the brush, and a soaring Verreaux's eagle silently scans for potential prey on the ground far below.

From open grasslands to woodlands, riparian forests and closed-canopy thickets, the Serengeti's rich variety of vegetation nourishes an incredible diversity of bird species, and the rhythms and sounds of its winged residents frame each day.

Surrounded by sound

The beauty starts before dawn, with the clear, melodious song of a single lark, soon joined by the cheery warbling of a morning thrush. As dawn paints the sky, the solitary notes grow into a chorus, and a crescendo of birdsong rises from the plains. It's as if the whole Earth is awakening in a glorious symphony of life, just as it must have done at the beginning of time.

Chirping, trilling and twittering is everywhere, joyously uplifting. Shortly after sunrise it reaches a

Right: The omnivorous superb starling can be spotted in the Serengeti

Below: A pack of African hunting dogs pursue wildebeest through the Serengeti dawn

Q&A

Why do you love Serengeti birding?
The park's environments are so diverse and different vegetation zones host a wide variety of species.

Which months are best?
November to March.

Throughout the day?
Birding is especially good in the morning and late afternoon.

Most amazing Serengeti birding?
Spotting the swamp flycatcher, black-headed gonolek, brown-throated weaver, brown-chested lapwing, red-chested sunbird and western banded snake eagle.

Do you have any tips for visitors?
Visit western Serengeti and Ndutu (which is in the Ngorongoro Conservation Area and runs into southeastern Serengeti), as these are the best birding locations.

Nuru Sanga, professional birder and Wilkinson Tours wildlife guide

© Jonathan Gregson / Lonely Planet; FotoRequest / Shutterstock

peak, before settling into a low, humming backdrop. In the heat of the afternoon, the birdsong quietens, before rising again in one final burst at sunset. With the onset of darkness, night sounds take over, punctuated by the chirring of nightjars and the whoop-whooping of owls.

Sentinels of the Serengeti

Just as the Serengeti's birds frame the day with their song, they also mark the cycles of life on the plains. It is the raptors, such as tawny and bateleur eagles, who seem to know first where the lions are, as they optimally position themselves above a pride.

A goshawk tracks a honey badger, while lappet-faced vultures wait in watchful attendance on migrating wildebeest herds. The stately secretary bird minces stiffly through the short grass, watching for snakes and lizards, while an inquisitive grey-breasted spurfowl picks its way along the roadside.

Right: Fischer's lovebird, a small parrot, resting on an acacia bush

Far right: An African fish eagle hunting in Tanzania

The seasons, too, play a role. In December and January, with banks of cloud moving darkly across the plains, the Serengeti's avian residents reach their peak, joined by great flocks of white storks and other migrants from the north. As the rains turn the savannah green and wash dust from the woodland leaves, breeding season starts. Green-and-orange Fischer's lovebirds, and many others, begin to build their nests, and the brightly coloured plumages of breeding males make birding in these months a special delight.

Don't Miss

→ **Spending a morning listening to the rhythmic rise and fall of birdsong**

→ **Seeing the sun rise over the Serengeti plains**

→ **Watching the kori bustard, Africa's heaviest flier, as it takes to the air**

Find Your Joy

Getting there

The closest air hub is Kilimanjaro International Airport, from where it's an hour to Arusha and another seven or so to the Serengeti by road (1½ to two hours via small plane). Serengeti's western corridor is easily reachable by road from Mwanza and Lake Victoria.

Accessibility

An increasing number of operators offer wheelchair-adapted vehicles, and centre safaris around the park's wheelchair-accessible camps. The Serengeti comes alive for visually impaired visitors with its ever-present symphony of sound. Specialist guides can help with bird-call identification.

When to go

Birding is good year-round, with the wetter months, particularly February and March, especially rewarding.

Further information
• Admission charge. No prebooking required, but accommodation bookings are recommended.
• Year-round.
• Lodges and tented camps throughout the park.
• www.tanzaniaparks. go.tz

Other Tanzanian Birding Sites

Rubondo Island National Park

This island-based park in Lake Victoria's southwestern corner is awash with birds and blanketed in tranquillity. Over 300 species have been identified, including African fish eagles and various herons, ibis, storks, kingfishers and cormorants, making Rubondo another of East Africa's prime birding destinations. Because the park receives only a trickle of visitors, you'll usually have it to yourself.

Don't miss

Taking a guided boat safari along the shoreline to see the birds from a different perspective, along with hippos and crocodiles.

Lake Natron

Large, alkaline Lake Natron, east of Serengeti National Park, is a major breeding ground for the lesser flamingo. From September to April, up to two million of these delicately hued birds fill the lake's shallows. This magnificent sight, combined with Natron's convenient location on the back route into Serengeti's Loliondo region, make it a fine birding destination.

Don't miss

Hiking to nearby waterfall of Ngare Sero, watching out for nesting vultures along the way.

Be awed by a million pink flamingos

 Wildlife wonder, prehistoric landscapes, powerful nature

 July to September & November to March

It's the smell that hits you first. A powerful, briny odour that strikes deep into the back of the nostrils and threatens to knock you out. How on earth, you might wonder, can a bird that moves with all the grace of a ballerina smell so much like a teenage boy's socks?

And that's the thing with flamingos. They're full of surprises and contradictions. For example, who would have guessed that the reason flamingos are pink is down to what they eat rather than because nature made them that colour?

Another surprising thing about flamingos is how they thrive in the caustic, soda-rich waters of Kenya's Lake Bogoria – an environment so extreme that most other creatures would quickly die here.

Admire the flamingo ballet
Despite the harsh environment – and the memorable odour – there's something ethereally beautiful about seeing a huge flock of flamingos crowding out Lake Bogoria, or one of East Africa's other Rift Valley soda lakes. From afar, the heat haze that rises off the salt-rimmed mudflats surrounding the lake turns everything into a milky blur. But closing in on the scene, the thorny acacias thin out and shapes take on a more solid dimension, until that smudge of pink takes the form of up to a million strutting flamingos.

Right: Lesser flamingos in flight

Below: Saline Lake Bogoria provides spirulina algae on which lesser flamingos feed

Q&A

Flamingos seem like high-maintenance birds – why do they keep moving from lake to lake?
They move from one lake to another because of rising and falling water levels. If the water is too deep, the algae they feed on disappears, so they move to a shallower lake.

And when you find the flamingo's lake of choice, is there a best time to be there?
Flamingos gather in big flocks all year, but November to March when the babies are present is a good time.

Rift Valley lakes aren't just about pink, leggy birds, are they? What are the other key birds to look out for?
There are over 200 bird species present, but look for white-billed buffalo weavers, red bishops and shoveler ducks.

Tiampati Manei, Kenyan wildlife photographer and bird expert

© Christian Nuebling / Shutterstock; Reto Buehler / Shutterstock; Steffen Foerster / Shutterstock; neil bowman/ Getty Images

Left: Some of the millions of lesser flamingos at Lake Bogoria; a pigment in the algae creates their pink hue

Right: A Verreaux's eagle owl surveys its domain

Why the odour?

With so much hypnotic action taking place in front of your eyes, you may almost forget the smell. But, if you lower your binoculars for a moment and take a deep breath, you might find yourself wondering just why such a glamorous bird smells so bad. And the answer is as unexpected as everything else about flamingos.

The algae which they spend all day feasting on is full of bacteria that produce hydrogen sulphide, sometimes known as 'sewer gas'. It's highly corrosive and very poisonous – unless you're a flamingo that is – and it's also one of the base chemicals in flatulence.

So, to put it indelicately, that teen-sock smell that greets anyone watching flamingos comes from those thousands of beautiful ballerina birds farting. A lot. Which is probably something that would endear them to any teenage boy!

Don't Miss

→ Being overpowered by the noise (and smell) of the flamingo flock

→ Watching out for eagles keen to make a snack of baby flamingos

→ Spying a rare greater kudu antelope in the lakeside woodlands

Most of the birds busy themselves with the eternal search for food, standing head down in the warm, shallow waters as they sweep their beaks back and forth to sieve up the algae that sustains them. But, as the sun starts to sink lazily to the west and the bubbles of volcanic gas rise up from the far shore, some of the flamingos form groups and, in their tutu-dress colours, they perform a delicate and perfectly coordinated dance that's more 'Flamingo Lake' than *Swan Lake*.

Find Your Joy

Getting there
Lake Bogoria is easily accessible by road from Nairobi – a 150-mile (240km) trip – but there's no public transport, so you'll need to hire a vehicle in Nairobi or Nakuru or join an organised safari. You're not allowed to walk in most of Lake Bogoria National Reserve, but you can get out of vehicles by the lake for a better view. Entry fees apply for visitors and vehicles, but guides are not mandatory.

Accessibility
There are no facilities within the reserve for travellers with limited mobility, but you can watch flamingos from your vehicle, across the broad mudflats.

When to go
Flamingos are very sensitive to changes in lake-water conditions and will leave if water levels rise or fall too much. In general, January is a prime month.

Further information
• Admission charge.
• Open year-round.
• No specialist facilities.
• No refreshments on-site.
• Accommodation in Lorwok, close to the reserve entrance.
• www.kws.go.ke

© Reto Buehler / Shutterstock; Gunter Nuyts / Shutterstock

Other Bird-Filled African Lakes

Lake Naivasha, Kenya

East Africa's Rift Valley lakes are split between freshwater and soda lakes. Lake Naivasha falls into the former category, which means that it has a very different kind of birdlife to Lake Bogoria. You won't spot flamingos here, but it's a great place to see huge and powerful African fish eagles alongside some 350 other recorded species.

Don't miss
The many other birds that gather on the lake, including fulvous whistling ducks, goliath herons and little grebes.

Lake Langano, Ethiopia

Kenya isn't the only East African country blessed with a string of Rift Valley lakes. Ethiopia, widely regarded as one of Africa's best birding destinations, also has a series of freshwater and soda lakes that attract huge quantities of birds. Freshwater Lake Langano is considered one of the best – and easiest – to visit.

Don't miss
Ticking off a Verreaux's eagle-owl, white-bellied go-away bird and Hemprich's hornbill.

Let the ostrich be your gateway into Africa's avian world

♡ Chance encounters, wonder, appreciation of nature

🕐 Year-round

BOTSWANA

In Botswana's Chobe National Park, wildlife encounters are inevitable – so much so that you might well see more than you anticipated just on the ride to your lodge. Covering more than 4500 sq miles (11,655 sq km) of woodlands and floodplains, Chobe is home to dozens of mammals and more than 450 species of birds. However, for many safari-goers, particularly first-timers, most of these birds don't get much attention – except for one: the ostrich.

Enter the big bird

With its long neck, relatively small head and disproportionately large legs, the ostrich is a truly peculiar creature that appears to have been conjured up by fantasy. It can stand taller than 10ft

(3m), with a wingspan of about 6.5ft (2m) and long legs that can take it over 43mph (70km/h), yet it cannot fly. And as this larger-than-life bird forages for its food – mostly plants and some small animals – it walks with an almost rhythmic, stalking strut, reminding us that birds are the living descendants of dinosaurs.

As the biggest bird on the planet, the ostrich is on everyone's safari checklist. But because ostriches are not as ubiquitous as antelopes or pachyderms, they need to be pursued with intention, relying partly on random luck – and it's during the doldrums of tracking them that other birds come into focus.

A safari-load of birdlife

Chobe's lesser-known birds are certainly not less interesting

Right: Male ostriches are the world's largest and heaviest birds

Below: A group of ostriches in Chone National Park

© Lasse Johansson / Shutterstock; Simon Eeman / Shutterstock; LouieLea / Shutterstock; Jonathan Gregson / Lonely Planet

Q&A

How do you track an ostrich?
We start in landscapes where we'd expect to find them – open areas and grasslands. If we notice their footprints, we can track their direction. You must consider the angle of the tracks – where their toes are pointing. But because they are so big and usually in open areas, most often you see them easily!

How do you track other birds?
Find and observe their habitat – surrounding trees, bushes and landscape. Look. Listen to their calls. Clear your mind, heighten your senses, be immersed and scan the surroundings with binoculars.

Why do you like watching Botswana's birds?
It's therapeutic. It relieves stress and anxiety – for me, at least! It's also incredibly rewarding; considering migratory birds, different plumages, gender differences and rituals.

Isaac Mpuchane, Desert & Delta Safaris specialist guide

than the ostrich. Each has some peculiarity that generates curiosity – like the kori bustard, which can reach 5ft (1.5m) tall and, while mostly ground-dwelling, has the ability to fly. In fact, it's the world's heaviest flying bird.

Similar in size is the marabou stork – but this dark-feathered 'undertaker bird' is not the charming white-plumed creature associated with newborns. It earned its nickname for its association with death and its habit of scavenging carcasses; even the distinctive clattering sound it makes with its bill sounds like a death rattle.

The appeal of Chobe's avian residents seems to increase as the birds get smaller. While it's common to see guinea fowl scurry out of the way of safari trucks, it is worth giving more attention to the knob-billed duck, with its distinctive bulging upper beak. And it's hard to ignore the hundreds of African songbirds flitting across the

Right: Southern carmine bee-eaters feed on other insects too

Far right: The Zambezi river is prime birdwatching habitat

landscape, many distinguishable by their strong colours – look out for lilac-breasted rollers, yellow-billed kites and glossy blue Cape starlings, to name but a few.

Of course, these feathered distractions take a backseat once an ostrich is spotted. There are thousands of ostriches in Chobe, so it's likely that you'll encounter one sooner or later. However, here's the thing about checking an ostrich off your must-see safari list – once you've come to appreciate all the other birds, that list just got a whole lot longer.

Don't Miss

→ Spotting a Ross's turaco in Linyanti Marsh

→ Observing flocks of African skimmers on the Chobe Riverfront

→ Watching southern carmine bee-eaters follow your truck in Savuti Marsh

Find Your Joy

Getting there
Chobe's closest airport is in Kasane, with daily flights from Johannesburg.

Alternative airports include Livingstone (Zambia) and Victoria Falls (Zimbabwe). You'll need to rent a 4WD to continue the journey (per-day vehicle fees will apply in the park), or go with a safari operator like Desert & Delta (www. desertdelta.com).

Accessibility
Birding in Botswana is

mostly done from safari trucks. Desert & Delta offer front seats to guests with limited mobility, as they're lower and easier to get in and out of. Its new lodge was also constructed with accessibility in mind.

When to go
You'll see birds year-round, but the green season (late October to early April), when migratory species

arrive, offers the most spectacular birding.

Further information
• Park admission charge (included on safaris).
• Year-round.
• No specialist facilities.
• Restaurants nearby in Kasane.
• Safari lodges and luxury camps in and around Chobe; campsites in the park.

© nwdph / Shutterstock; Philip Lee Harvey / Lonely Planet

Other Bird-Rich African Parks

Lower Zambezi National Park, Zambia

The Lower Zambezi section of this mighty river serves as the border between Zambia and Zimbabwe, and is another haven for birds. Keep eyes peeled for distinctive species, such as the long-toed African jacana, Lilian's lovebird (a parrot species), the long-tailed Meves's starling, white-breasted and reed cormorants, and Verreaux's eagle-owl, the largest owl in Africa.

Don't miss

Listening to the distinct, hypnotic call of the Cape dove.

Nyungwe Forest National Park, Rwanda

While Rwanda may be best known for the gorillas of Volcanoes National Park, birders will truly appreciate Nyungwe. Set in the country's southwest, within the Albertine Rift, it's home to 17 endemic bird species, including the bright orange Kivu ground thrush and the multicoloured regal sunbird. If you're lucky, you may spot the elusive and endangered Congo bay owl.

Don't miss

Seeing the iconic red, green and blue Rwenzori turaco.

Meet the Mauritius kestrel as it soars back from the brink of oblivion

 Rare encounters, conservation successes, endemic species

 September to February

MAURITIUS

Hiking trails tiptoe across the flanks of Vallée de Ferney, amid the Bambou Mountains. Here, vigilant visitors might spot a species that was, until recently, the planet's most endangered bird: the Mauritius kestrel.

With luck, you'll hear this spectacular speckled raptor first, as it soars through the rainforest hunting dragonflies and geckos. The male makes long, shrill calls when arriving back in his territory, while the female has a lower-pitched voice. When food passes between breeding pairs, their meals are punctuated by an affectionate chittering chatter.

Lessons of loss

Located 1100 lonely miles (1770km) east of Madagascar, Mauritius is a fleck of terra firma in the immense Indian Ocean. The island's idyllic coral-reef-encircled coastline, turquoise lagoons and verdant, volcanically sculpted hinterland has long exerted a pull on explorers, traders, smugglers, pirates, nature-chasers and newlyweds, but behind the beaches and luxury hotels, Mauritius is haunted by the ghosts of its former inhabitants.

Evolution produced some extraordinary endemic flora and fauna on this isolated isle – including the dodo, which dawdled predator-free through the ebony forests until seafaring humans landed. Famished sailors, en route to India and the Spice Islands, delighted in the discovery of this meaty flightless bird, and by 1662 it was extinct.

The dodo has achieved a form of unfortunate immortality by becoming an icon of extinction, but some of its feathered compatriots have come scarily close to following it into oblivion.

Right: The rare Mauritius kestrel hunts among trees

Below: Chamarel Falls in the Black River Gorges National Park

© Jonathan Stokes / Lonely Planet; Daniel Danckwerts / Shutterstock; Chris Moody / Shutterstock

Q&A

Is the future of the Mauritius kestrel now secure?
It should be safe from extinction, as long as nest boxes are maintained.

Give us some tips on how to spot a Mauritius kestrel in the wild?
You have the best chance of seeing them in Vallée de Ferney and Ebony Forest. Look during the day, between 8am and 4pm, especially November to December, when the male hunts nonstop to feed the brood. Ebony Forest offers birdwatching tours, where guides accompany visitors, providing details about birds and helping find them.

As the former MWF Kestrel Project coordinator, can you describe how you feel about the species?
The Mauritius kestrel has recently been declared the national bird of Mauritius. I feel proud that my work has contributed to its survival. It is an iconic bird and a symbol of hope for conservation.

Denis Li Lung Hok, Ebony Forest kestrel expert

Left: Mauritius' pink pigeon is also on the verge of extinction, due to inbreeding

Right: The challenging karst landscapes of Madagascar

It was saved by a desperate rescue mission, launched by an international collective of conservationists, including Gerald Durrell, who cofounded the Mauritian Wildlife Foundation (MWF). Now, around 300 Mauritius kestrels live in forest reserves around Vallée de Ferney near Mahebourg, and in the Black River Gorges National Park and Ebony Forest in southwest Mauritius. And the pink pigeon population has bounced back too.

These and other endemic species – including the echo parakeet and Mascarene paradise flycatcher – are observed and protected by ecotourism teams comprising young locals dedicated to preventing the remnants of their natural heritage going in the direction of the dodo. And now visitors, instead of bringing destruction, can play a positive role too; by supporting conservation projects while chasing the joyous sight of a Mauritius kestrel in flight.

Don't Miss

→ Tiptoeing through the Vallée de Ferney, listening for Mauritius kestrels

→ Spotting bountiful birds, flying foxes and giant tortoises in Black River Gorges National Park

→ Seeing sunrise over the southwest's Seven Coloured Earths and Chamarel Falls

The magnificent Mauritius kestrel came the closest to catastrophe.

Back from the brink
During the 1950s and '60s, Mauritius was doused with DDT in an attempt to destroy malaria-carrying mosquitoes – but the chemical also made many birds infertile, affecting multiple species, including the native kestrel and the pink pigeon, a direct relative of the dodo. By the early 1970s, the Mauritius kestrel was hovering on the very edge of extinction, with a wild population of just four.

Find Your Joy

Getting there
Sir Seewoosagur Ramgoolam International Airport is on Mauritius' southeast coast near Mahebourg, close to Vallée de Ferney (www. ferney.mu). Black River Gorges National Park (https://npcs.govmu.org) and Ebony Forest (www. ebonyforest.com) are in the southwest, but the island is only 30 miles (50km) across. The best way to visit nature reserves is by rental car, taxi or minibus; guided birding tours are available.

Accessibility
You can explore the national park, Vallée de Ferney and Ebony Forest on foot or by car. Some walkways will be challenging if you have limited mobility, but visitor centres are accessible.

When to go
The best time to see the Mauritius kestrel is during summer (September/ October through to January/February). The pink pigeon can be spotted at any time.

Further information
• Admission charge for Ebony Forest and Vallée de Ferney; the national park is free.
• Open year-round.
• No specialist facilities.
• Lodge and restaurant in Vallée de Ferney.

© Daniel Danckwerts / Shutterstock; Justin Foulkes / Lonely Planet

Other Indian Ocean Island Encounters

Vallée de Mai Nature Reserve, Seychelles

Amid heavily fruited coco de mer palm trees in the Vallée de Mai Nature Reserve on the island of Praslin, you can spot the rare Seychelles black parrot. Unique to Praslin, this funereally feathered parrot is the national bird of the Republic of the Seychelles.

Don't miss
Scanning Vallée de Mai's thief palms to spot the endemic Seychelles blue pigeon, bulbuls and the incandescently hot-coloured sunbird.

Réserve Spéciale Ankarana, Madagascar

In the ancient limestone landscape of the Réserve Spéciale Ankarana in northern Madagascar, something curious happens. Here, several different species of birds – including the paradise flycatcher, sunbirds, greenbuls, bulbuls and vangas – can be observed foraging together, in an unusual practice that's thought to offer greater returns and improved protection from predators.

Don't miss
Harrier hawks hunting crowned lemurs across the reserve's dry forests and karst plateaus.

See sooty falcons hunt amid Nabataean ruins

 World wonders, temples and talons, migratory raptors

 May to October

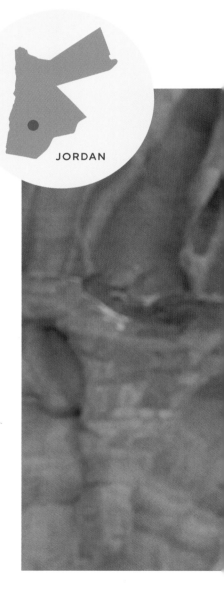

JORDAN

Morning sunlight probes the sepia fissures of the Jordanian desert, as though prying open the Earth's crust. In a deep wadi (valley), perched atop an ancient pediment, a fledgling sooty falcon (*Falco concolor*) shakes out its inexperienced wings. Nearby, its charcoal-coloured parents, their talons shining a bright yellow, scan a cluster of tombs and temples; these vast, reverential structures, carved directly into the canyon walls by skilled artisans, provide enticingly sheltered nesting sites for birds.

Bird encounters in a lost kingdom

As day breaks, flocks of tourists, as well as local Bedouin leading their mules and camels, will flood into the depths of Petra, often unaware of the birds nesting and hunting in plain sight. One of the New Seven Wonders of the World, this former Nabataean city dates back at least 2300 years, but a perfect storm of war, desertification and earthquakes meant it was largely abandoned by the 8th century CE. Secluded and well concealed, the ruins of Petra faded from the memory of all but local Bedouin custodians, lying unknown to the outside world for over a thousand years.

Petra's main entrance is via a steep-sided tectonic rift called the Siq. It's a 20-minute amble through narrow, sinewy rock, at the end of which rises the majestic Al-Khazneh, the Treasury. In years when they deign to nest in Petra, sooty falcons often raise their young nearby. While most visitors are simply awed by the spectacle of the building, bird lovers will also register the falcon's squeaky

Right: The Treasury at Petra is known locally as Al-Khazneh,

Below: The deadly elegance of Jordan's sooty falcon

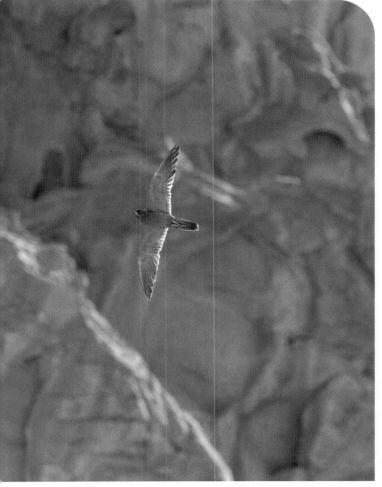

© Marco Valentini / Alamy Stock Photo; Tom Mackie / Lonely Planet; Nature Picture Library / Alamy Stock Photo

Q&A

Where do Jordan's sooty falcons live?
From the Dead Sea rift margins down to Wadi Rum. I saw them nesting just beside the Treasury in Petra; just after you exit the Siq, they were right there.

Why there, of all places?
They love the sandstone cliffs!

And the sightseeing, no doubt?
Or the feeding. All they need is some big insects and migratory passerines.

Hardy little things, aren't they?
Yes. They can live in the most arid areas. In the Sahara they even nest beneath big rocks.

They must be easy to miss amid Petra's many temples?
They're very active during the day. They also call a lot, similar to a kestrel – a high-pitched trilling. If they're around, they're not difficult to spot.

Dr Fares Khoury, Jordan BirdWatch (JBW) cofounder

trill, reverberating off the wadi walls. That's if the occasional belch of an ornery camel, the whinny of a mule, or the clop of hooves gently navigating timeworn steps doesn't steal your attention first.

Wadi wonderland, desert specialists

Being at the intersection of Africa, Asia and Europe, migratory birds regularly pass through the region, with smaller species, passerines in particular, frequently touching down in these wadis to rest and refuel. The rose-hued sandstone cliffs are pockmarked with weathered dimples and honeycombed *tafoni* – eroded cavities, scraped out by the elements – offering small mammals and birds shelter from the relentless sun.

You'll soon notice how dry everything is here, as the wind whips at the dust and the sun bakes the landscape. But the pleasure of watching birds

Right: The Sinai rosefinch is Jordan's national bird

Far right: Eleonora's falcon can be sighted across the Mediterranean

adapted to live in such harsh conditions, amid such majestic surroundings, also provides a deeper degree of appreciation for the 40,000 humans who once inhabited Petra.

Now, only the hardiest creatures thrive here, such as Jordan's national bird, the Sinai rosefinch, whose pink plumage helps it camouflage perfectly against the Rose City's sandstone. Unless, of course, it catches the keen eye of a sooty falcon, eager to provide an extra meal for its chick, to fuel its first migration south for the winter.

Don't Miss

→ **Sipping Bedouin tea while overlooking Petra's Monastery**

→ **Spotting small mammals like the rock hyrax sunning on the cliffs**

→ **Glimpsing the flash of a sooty falcon swooping after its prey**

Find Your Joy

Getting there
A daily JETT bus connects tourist town Wadi Musa, at Petra's gates, to Amman; local buses from Aqaba run four times a day. Airports at Aqaba and Amman are served by international flights.

Accessibility
Previously, Petra visits required lots of walking and steps, or hiring an (often poorly treated) donkey or camel; but in 2022 a small fleet of electric 'club cars' was unveiled, greatly improving access and reducing the need for beasts of burden.

When to go
Sooty falcons return to Jordan in late April, only becoming more active in August, when they start nesting and egg laying. This is Jordan's hottest month, but they remain active until mid-October, the best time to visit. By mid-November, the falcons are gone.

Further information
• Admission charge. No booking required.
• Open daily from 6am until 4pm (6pm in summer).
• Bring water. Cafe and restaurant on-site.
• Hotels in Wadi Musa near the Siq entrance.
• www.visitpetra.jo

Other Great Spots to See Falcons

Eleonora's falcons, Greece

The sooty falcon is a Red Sea and Gulf specialist; its closest relative, Eleonora's falcon(*Falco eleonorae*) is a Mediterranean maestro. The Greek island of Tílos, roughly 13 miles (21km) from mainland Turkey, as the falcon flies, is home to the world's largest breeding population of Eleonora's falcons, although you'll find them across most Med islands as far as the Balearics.

Don't miss

Watching Eleonora's falcons hunting at the Venetian fortress presiding over Megálo Horió village.

Saker falcons, United Arab Emirates

Prehistoric petroglyphs found in Iran suggest a Middle Eastern falconry heritage dating back 9000 years. As one of the larger members of its genus, saker falcons (*Falco cherrug*) are valued for their speed and hunting abilities, but are now endangered. In Abu Dhabi, however, the conservation and reintroduction efforts of the Environment Agency seeks to protect these migratory raptors.

Don't miss

Touring the Abu Dhabi Falcon Hospital, where sick birds are nursed back to health.

Stroll the city to seek out Ottoman-era bird palaces

 Urban walks, history, hidden treasures

 Year-round

TÜRKIYE

When the Italian novelist Edmondo De Amicis visited Constantinople in the 1870s, he found a place where 'mosque and grove, ancient wall and garden, palace and courtyard, are full of song, of the cheerful sound of twittering and chirping. Everywhere there is the rush of wings, everywhere the busy, active little lives go on.'

The 'veneration and affection' for birds that De Amicis noted among the human residents of what's now called İstanbul can still be seen today in some of the city's tiniest architectural treasures: dozens of centuries-old stone, brick and tile birdhouses – some extravagant enough to please a picky sultan. Near pigeon-flocked Beyazıt Meydanı on İstanbul's historic peninsula, a multistorey stone birdhouse – resplendent with

delicate latticework and flanked by two mini minarets – sits under the eaves of the 18th-century Seyyid Hasan Paşa Madrasa. Below the seagulls swooping noisily over Taksim Meydanı in the Beyoğlu district, bits of twigs poke out of two avian duplexes perched serenely on the entry to the Taksim Maksemi, a structure built in 1732 to distribute water to the city's growing population.

Soul of the city

Birds are revered in some Islamic and pre-Islamic traditions as symbols of the human soul, and taking care of animals was regarded as a good deed by devout Muslims in the Ottoman era. After they conquered Constantinople in 1453, the Ottoman sultans erected grand public buildings that still lend a rich architectural flourish to İstanbul's older neighbourhoods

Right: Birds nesting on the city's Mihrimah Sultan Mosque

Below: Look up at the Laleli Mosqueto spot other Ottoman birdhouses

Q&A

Are there really many birds here?
İstanbul is actually an excellent place to see birds. One retired teacher who goes birding every day near the Fatih Mosque has seen about 200 species.

Wow, where do they all live?
We're not very tidy with our buildings, so there are lots of gaps and hollows where birds can build their nests.

Were these fancy old birdhouses practical, or just pretty?
The people who made them really thought about what birds needed. And having them on buildings that the sultan commissioned sent a big signal to the rest of society too.

Best place in İstanbul to birdwatch?
That question is really against the whole idea of urban birding – we don't need to go anywhere special; if you want to see birds, just look around where you already are.

Kerem Ali Boyla, ecologist and İstanbul urban birder

© Joshua Bruce Allen / Shutterstock; Yusuf Tatliturk / Shutterstock; Atakan Divitlioglu / Shutterstock

Left: A bird's eye view of Taksim Square in İstanbul

Right: A grey heron cools off at İstanbul's coast

Practical & stylish

No matter how stunning, these birdhouses weren't just for looks. From the most basic to the most lavish, they were carefully designed: oriented to block strong sun or harsh winds, placed at a protective height and equipped with entry holes small enough to keep out predatory larger birds while sheltering sparrows, swallows, doves and goldfinches.

This unique urban heritage remains largely unsung, however, and many birdhouses have fallen victim to new construction or neglect. Those that have survived don't always receive the regular cleaning they need to allow new nests to flourish inside. But for anyone who takes the time to raise their eyes up while wandering the city and look for them, these small symbols of coexistence provide poignant reminders that no environment is too urban to be shared with other species.

Don't Miss

→ Scouring walls for birdhouses at Ayazma and Yeni Valide Mosques

→ Sipping a *çay* (tea) upstairs inside the Büyük Yeni Han

→ Snagging a sighting of alpine swifts swirling over Taksim Meydanı

– and the walls of these mosques, madrasas (traditional schools for Islamic religious instruction), hammams and *hans* (a kind of urban caravanserai for commercial use) often included spaces for the city's winged inhabitants. What started off as simple holes in the sides of buildings developed into intricate, sometimes fantastically whimsical *serçe sarayları* (sparrow palaces) or *kuş köşkleri* (bird villas) designed to replicate in miniature the latest architectural fashion of the day, complete with staircases, balconies, columns and cupolas.

Find Your Joy

Getting there
Starting from the Spice Bazaar near the Eminönü tram stop, the easy 2-mile (3km) walk to the Fatih Mosque passes at least 10 birdhouse-adorned buildings. On the city's Anatolian (Asian) side, the Yeni Valide Mosque and its elaborate, dome-topped birdhouses are right behind the Üsküdar metro/Marmaray station and a short walk from the ferry docks.

Accessibility
Though most of İstanbul's historic birdhouses can be seen from the street and require no special entrance fees, the city's crowded and not always well-maintained sidewalks can be difficult to navigate for travellers with mobility challenges.

When to go
April to May and September to October are typically the most reliable months for good strolling weather (clear, dry, not too hot) in İstanbul.

Further information
• Free to visitors.
• Year-round.
• No specialist facilities.
• There are cafes, restaurants and accommodation options throughout İstanbul.

© yusufyilmaz / Shutterstock; Sipa US / Alamy Stock Photo

Other İstanbul Birding Experiences

White storks, Princes' Islands

Hundreds of thousands of white storks fly over İstanbul each year as part of their annual migration between Europe and Africa. The awe-inspiring sight of huge flocks of the birds soaring through the skies is especially dramatic from the Princes' Islands in the Marmara Sea during their September return to warmer climes.

Don't miss
The silver gulls that chase ferries to the islands in hopes of nabbing a tossed piece of bread.

Grey herons, Gülhane Park

Some six dozen large nests sway at the tops of the towering plane trees that line the main path through Gülhane Park, once part of the royal grounds of next-door Topkapı Palace. These perches come to raucous life in the spring when the park's resident grey heron colony goes into breeding mode.

Don't miss
The gracefully long-necked adult birds gliding back to their nests.

Americas & Antarctica

© Ondrej Prosicky / Shutterstock

Cruise coral keys to spy pink roseate spoonbills

 Boating adventures, urban escapes, island bliss

 November to April

USA

Despite its proximity to Miami, Florida's richly biodiverse Biscayne National Park feels like a different world entirely – and as 95% percent of it is underwater, getting out to see its feathered residents is half of the fun. And from shoreside Dante Fascell Visitor Center – draped in tropical hardwood hammocks and visited by white-crowned pigeons, wood storks and mangrove cuckoos that seemingly chirp hello to guests – you can hop on a boat to experience the park's true isolation and every-shade-of-blue bliss.

Chugging through a slight chop kicked up by the humid, salty breeze, you might catch sight of brown pelicans, white ibis and blue herons sunbathing on the channel markers; below the waves lie other creatures to complement your birding trek, from sea turtles splashing by to gently gliding manatees. But the real prize is sighting a roseate spoonbill, which is as quintessential a Sunshine State bird as you'll find. It's not uncommon to see one gliding low above Biscayne Bay on bubblegum-pink wings, perhaps slowing to dip its white head in the water for a fish snack under the always-beating sun.

Roseate renaissance

The park's shallow waters, teeming with small fish and crustaceans, make a prime feeding ground for the roseate spoonbill, but while its population is strong in Florida – upwards of 2400 breeding birds in recent counts – the situation hasn't always been so rosy. In the early 1800s, their wing feathers were in demand as material for making hand-fans and for accent

Right: A mangrove cuckoo in Miami-Dade County

Below: In recent years, the roseate spoonbill has expanded its range into Georgia, South Carolina and beyond

© Donyanedomam / Getty Images; Agami Photo Agency / Shutterstock; simonkr / Getty Images

Q&A

What makes a trip to the barrier islands so spectacular?
You have the potential of seeing a lot of birds from the Caribbean not usually found in South Florida, some drifting from the Bahamas, Cuba and all places in between. These barrier islands or Miami are usually their first spot, making for such a unique mix.

Any visitor no-no's for Biscayne National Park?
If you don't go during the winter months, it can be very, very buggy. We're talking about mosquitos, no-see-ums and anything that bites. The summer months on Elliott Key are almost unbearable.

Okay, if I don't have a boat, what's the best way to get around the park?
I'd encourage you to look at the park's approved outfitters on their website. They do a lot of eco-type adventures, snorkelling, kayaking, paddleboarding and walking tours, all of which are quintessential experiences in the park, too.

Marc Kramer, Birding by Bus founder

Left: A canoe trip on Biscayne Bay Lagoon is a great way to spot birds

Right: The Everglades' rivers of grass attract vast numbers of birds

Offshore wonders at Biscayne

Boca Chita and Elliott Keys are the most visited of the park's coral islets, sitting approximately 7 miles (11km) offshore – or an hourlong boat ride from the Visitor Centre. Upon arrival at this chain of barrier islands – fun fact – you'll be engulfed in the longest stretch of mangrove forest on the US East Coast. And within, you'll find choruses of chirpers perched in the treetops, awaiting listening ears and watchful eyes.

Beyond pops of colour in the form of yellow-throated warblers and messy-haired green herons, the islands are also a first stop for Caribbean guests, such as the Antillean nighthawk, with its distinctive white-striped wings, and the hefty Bahama mockingbird. Seeing the pink roseate spoonbills alongside such absorbing avian characters, amid a backdrop of lush greenery and sparkling blue waters, is a uniquely tropical birding experience.

Don't Miss

→ **Spotting roseate spoonbills nesting on the keys**

→ **Hearing mangrove cuckoos gaw-gaw-gaw-ing around the tree-ringed visitor centre**

→ **Watching brown booby families napping on channel markers in the bay**

pieces on hats; unsurprisingly, spoonbill numbers plummeted as a result. But with the creation of the national park system and preservation areas in South Florida in the mid-1900s, nest sites – and the roseate spoonbill population – began to flourish once again.

Today, initiatives like the Biscayne Bay Coastal Wetlands Project help preserve the roseate spoonbill and other bird species by endeavours such as building pump stations to reduce freshwater discharge into the bay and Biscayne National Park.

Find Your Joy

Getting there
Flying into Miami International Airport, it's around 43 miles' (69km) drive south to Homestead,

from where trolley-buses run to the visitor centre on weekends from January to March. By public transport, take the Miami Metrorail south from the airport to Dadeland, then bus 38 to Homestead.

Accessibility
The Dante Fascell Visitor Center has designated parking spots for drivers with disabilities,

wheelchair-friendly picnic tables and accessible bathrooms; its Convoy Point Jetty Walk is wheelchair-accessible.

When to go
November to April is the nesting season for many coastal birds, including roseate spoonbills. It's outside the Atlantic hurricane season, and temperatures are pleasant

compared with summer heat, with highs averaging 27°C (80°F).

Further information
• Park entry is free.
• Open year-round.
• No specialist facilities.
• Dining options in Homestead.
• Campsites in the park, and hotels in Florida City and Homestead.
• www.nps.gov

© Sandra Foyt / Shutterstock; Justin Foulkes / Lonely Planet

Other South Florida Destinations

Everglades National Park

About the size of Rhode Island, the Everglades is Florida's most prized swampland. From the Shark Valley entrance (35 miles/56km west of Miami International Airport), you can walk, cycle or take a tram along a 15-mile (24km) paved loop to see roseate spoonbills, great white herons and wood storks, while alligators loom in the shallow trailside waters.

Don't miss
Spotting pink, stilt-legged American flamingos in the shallow lagoons and estuaries.

Larry & Penny Thompson Memorial Park

Adjacent to Zoo Miami in southwest Miami, and within the Richmond Pinelands, this 270-acre (109-hectare) park, with its central freshwater lake, is a good spot to catch sight of numerous wintering and migrant songbirds as well as scaly-breasted munias; look out, too, for the always-defensive brown thrasher, an avid protector of its nest.

Don't miss
Scouring the park's palms for the orange-and-black plumage of the eastern towhee.

Zoom in on Zapata to see the world's smallest bird

♡ Rare encounters, migratory visitors, tropical tranquillity

🕐 November to May

CUBA

You'll usually hear it before you see it – the sound of the Cuban trogon, its repeated staccato-like call, 'to-co-ro-ro, to-co-ro-ro', resounding across the forest. Clear and melodious, the song invariably leads you to the bird itself, half hidden in high branches of dense tropical foliage, its vivid red, white and blue plumage the same colours as the Cuban flag.

The trogon, or tocororo as it's onomatopoeically known here, is Cuba's national bird and one of 27 endemic species in the archipelago. Although the tocororo is present in significant numbers countrywide, the best place to admire its iridescent colours is in the Ciénaga de Zapata, a national park, Unesco Biosphere Reserve and internationally acclaimed birder's paradise on Cuba's south coast.

Viva Zapata!
Famed as the place where the Cold War nearly got dangerously hot at the Bay of Pigs in 1961, the Zapata Peninsula is a tranquil backwater these days, where crocodiles bask in briny swamps and the quavering sound of birdsong invites you to be a privileged observer at a nature show that has been going on, irrespective of human presence, for time immemorial.

This flat, shoe-shaped peninsula jutting into the Caribbean shelters over a dozen ecosystems and harbours well over half of Cuba's estimated 350 bird species, including 23 of the 27 endemics. Mostly devoid of human habitation, Zapata is considered one of the Caribbean's last remaining wildernesses, replete with swamps, mangroves, salt flats, savannah and thick semi-deciduous woodland.

Right: The Cuban trogon is the national bird of Cuba

Below: The Zapata swamp, prime birding habitat

Q&A

Favourite place to observe birds?
Sopillar (a small community east of Playa Larga) and Santo Tomás, where I'm from and where I started out as an ornithologist.

Top bee hummingbird spot?
Sopillar, Hondones and Santo Tomás. It's also easy to spot them in various private gardens. The ponasi (firebush) is an important plant frequented by hummingbirds.

Have you ever seen a Zapata rail?
I once sighted a rail during a study expedition in a peatland area, but it was impossible to photograph due to the density of the existing vegetation. I have also recorded a sighting of a potoo de Jamaica (northern potoo), which was a very important experience for me.

Biggest birding draws for visitors?
Zapata wren, Zapata sparrow, Zapata rail, bee hummingbird, tocororo, Cuban tody and all the different owls.

Orestes Martínez, alias Chino Zapata, birdwatching guide

The soul of the peninsula is its humid wetlands, bisected by the snaking Río Hatiguanico and crisscrossed by a network of marshy canals, embellished with water lilies and lined by sawgrass and slender palms. This watery maze protects copious bird species, including several very rare endemics. The critically endangered Zapata rail, said to hide in the dense sawgrass and barely able to fly, has only been seen once since 1970 and never photographed. Less elusive, but always exciting to witness, is the tiny Zapata wren, its trill-like call warbling over the freshwater marshes where it nests.

From flamingos to hummingbirds

Biodiversity is Zapata's hallmark. On the south-coast salt flats of Las Salinas, red-pink flamingos shovel their bills through silty lagoons searching for prawns. From national park hub Playa Larga, a rough road forges west

Right: A tiny bee hummingbird feeding on nectar

Far right: The American flamingos of Cayo Coco are recovering after Hurricane Irma

to the tiny swamp village of Santo Tomás, where local *cienagueros* (swamp people) in wooden boats punt birders along narrow canals overhung with branches.

Santo Tomás is a prime spot to see the bee hummingbird (zunzuncito), the world's tiniest bird, measuring a mere 2.5in (6.4cm) head-to-tail. It's mesmerising to witness this industrious little creature that dips its slender bill into up to 1500 flowers a day, its wings beating at 200 times per second. For many birders, it's Zapata's smallest – and biggest – draw.

Don't Miss

→ **Seeing flocks of elegant pink flamingos in the brackish waters at Las Salinas**

→ **Following the distinctive call of a tocororo**

→ **Spying a zunzuncito feeding on a firebush**

Find Your Joy

Getting there

Zapata public transport only runs as far as the small beach community of Playa Larga: to see anything of the *ciénaga* (swamp) proper, visit as part of a tour or with your own wheels. Daily Viazul buses (www.viazul.wetransp.com) run from Havana to Playa Larga.

Accessibility

Rural Cuba is not well-designed for accessibility, although the generosity and help of local people goes a long way. In a decent rental car, you can drive to the popular birding spots of Las Salinas and Santo Tomás.

When to go

Numerous migratory birds from North America winter here, making November to May prime birding season.

Further information

• Guided tours only within the protected area. These can be organised at the national park office in Playa Larga or with Orestes Martínez (www.cubabirdguide.com). Fees apply. Book in advance.
• Open year-round.
• Specialist birdwatching guides.
• Private restaurants, and rooms to rent, in Playa Larga and neighbouring Caletón.

Other Cuban Birding Hot-spots

Soroa

The 'Rainbow of Cuba', hilly Soroa, west of Havana, is well stocked with colourful birdlife. Home to Cuba's largest *orquideario* (orchid garden), the region attracts several endemic species, including the tocororo, the bright-red and green Cuban tody, and the Cuban green woodpecker. Its forested slopes, rich in biodiverse flora, are also a good place to observe rare migrant warblers.

Don't miss

Local trails to a mirador (lookout) and the Salto del Arco Iris waterfall.

Cayo Coco

Named for the American white ibis ('coco' in Cuba), a slender wader with a reddish downcurved bill, Cayo Coco is the archipelago's fourth-largest island, a flat eyebrow-shaped key covered in mangrove swamps, brackish lagoons and low tropical woodland. Connected to the main island via a 17-mile (27km) causeway, it has been developed as a resort enclave, but this hasn't blunted its birdwatching allure.

Don't miss

Seeing pelicans, piping plovers and the largest concentration of American flamingos in the western hemisphere.

Admire giant flocks on British Columbia's Pacific Flyway

 Mudflats, sea air, murmuration patterns

 November to March

CANADA

As avian shows go, it's a remarkable spectacle. A lone peregrine falcon flies low above the braided mouth of the Fraser River, its attention focused on a huge flock of dunlins feeding on the rippled mudflats below.

Alerted to impending danger, the gathered birds lift their wings nervously before taking off en masse in a tight formation that oscillates in shape and direction, etching kaleidoscopic patterns in the air like iron filings swirling around a magnet.

A migratory rest-stop

These distinctive flock movements, or murmurations, are played out by thousands-strong groups of shorebirds to confuse predatory raptors and provide protection through strength in numbers. They're a common sight at the mouth of the Fraser River, just south of Vancouver, where BC's mightiest watercourse empties into the Strait of Georgia.

Herein lies western Canada's most productive bird habitat, a silt-rich river delta that supports around 1.7 million annual avian visitors, from plump western sandpipers to elegant red-throated loons. Birds use the estuary as an important stopover on the so-called Pacific Flyway, a 3977-mile (6400km) aerial route between Alaska and Patagonia that connects Arctic breeding grounds with winter foraging sites further south.

Tripod-wielding ornithologists arrive here to experience birdwatching that's less about sleuthing for rare species, and more about observing giant flocks of migrating shorebirds painting graceful patterns in the sky, with Vancouver's North Shore Mountains shimmering behind.

Right: Visiting George C Reifel Migratory Bird Sanctuary

Below: A flock of dunlin are harassed by an eagle at the Fraser River delta

© Feng Yu / Shutterstock; JT8 / Shutterstock; Voodison328 / Shutterstock

Q&A

Favourite birdwatching place?
The George C Reifel Sanctuary. The diversity of birds there is outstanding, and there is a good chance of seeing locally rare species. The trails wind through a variety of habitats making each visit a fresh experience.

Most iconic species and why?
The bald eagle. Once close to extirpation, populations have rebounded to the extent that they are commonly seen most of the year. Dunlin and western sandpiper (species of shorebirds that occur seasonally in huge numbers), and snow geese wintering from Russia, are other spectacular birds to watch.

Rarest bird seen?
The curlew sandpiper.

Any advice for first-time birders?
Spotting shorebirds and waterfowl depends on the season and the tides. Check tide tables and look on EBird (www.ebird.org) to see seasonal bird alerts for estuary hotspots.

Anne Murray, birdwatcher and Delta Naturalists Society member

Left: Feeding black-capped chickadees in George C Reifel Migratory Bird Sanctuary

Right: Western sandpipers and dunlin resting

and boardwalks harbour 192 regular species, from saw-whet owls to hummingbirds. Various hides, lookouts and towers offer tempting snapshots of nesting bald eagles and sandhill cranes.

At the southern end of the delta, Boundary Bay's mudflats are arguably the best location to witness the Fraser's dramatic murmurations, as giant flocks of dunlins and sandpipers enact their aerial stunts. With the wind in your face and the ocean sparkling like crumpled foil in the background, there's no finer place to feel at one with the dynamic forces of nature.

On the delta's southern shores, White Rock Pier protrudes 1313ft (400m) into Semiahmoo Bay, allowing sufficient vantage to spot the migratory loons that winter on the Pacific Coast: the common, the sleek Pacific and the smaller red-throated loon (which has shed its distinctive rust-coloured markings by the time it stops by here in the autumn).

Don't Miss

→ **Spotting red-throated loons off the end of White Rock Pier**

→ **Watching massed murmurations in Boundary Bay**

→ **Exploring the trails and lookout towers of the George C Reifel Sanctuary**

Delta islands and mudflats

One of the delta's prime observation points is Iona Island, a regional park adjacent to Vancouver Airport. Here, reedy ponds provide a habitat for insect-chasing tree swallows, while a pair of 2.5-mile-long (4km) spits poking into the Strait of Georgia lie beneath the flight path of landing jets and noisy flocks of snow geese.

For rarer species, head 6 miles (10km) south to Westham Island's more sheltered George C Reifel Migratory Bird Sanctuary, where a network of paths, dykes

Find Your Joy

© Dau / Shutterstock; Danita Delimont / Alamy Stock Photo.

Getting there
Iona Island and the George C Reifel Migratory Bird Sanctuary are accessible by car. Boundary Bay and White Rock Pier are reachable on the public bus system from Vancouver.

Accessibility
The George C Reifel Sanctuary has several wheelchair-accessible trails and lookouts. White Rock Pier is accessible to wheelchairs and pushchairs. Iona Island's gravel causeways are flat and obstacle-free.

When to go
From November to March, when birds fly south from the Arctic for winter.

Further information
• The George C Reifel Sanctuary has an $8 entry fee and must be booked in advance. All the other areas are free.
• Open year-round.
• Hides and a viewing tower available at the George C Reifel Sanctuary.
• There are cafes and restaurants around White Rock pier and in Crescent Beach near Boundary Bay.
• Numerous hotels in Richmond, near Vancouver Airport.
• www. reifelbirdsanctuary.com

Other US River Deltas

Copper River Delta, Alaska

Just east of Cordova, the Copper River Delta is home to the biggest contiguous wetlands on North America's Pacific Coast, and sees the largest avian migration in the US; some five million shorebirds (including the entire global population of western sandpipers) pass through each spring.

Don't miss
The Shorebird Festival every May, when international experts lead field trips into the delta's wild mix of muskeg and mudflats.

Grays Harbor National Wildlife Refuge, Washington

One of the most important rest stops for migrating shorebirds navigating the Pacific Flyway, Grays Harbor sits at the mouth of the Chehalis River, and has registered over 300 species of bird, from huge flocks of sandpipers and dunlins to long-billed dowitchers and semipalmated plovers. May's Shorebird Festival coincides with the spring migration.

Don't miss
Spotting from the Sandpiper Trail, which cuts across a salt marsh via a boardwalk.

Admire bald eagles up in Alaska's thermals

 Wilderness, symbolism, statistics in flight

 May to September

USA

Portrayed on Greek and Roman medals, coins, flags and buildings, eagles have been a symbol of imperial power and authority since time immemorial. However, one – the bald eagle – garners even more respect and attention. Since 1782, it has been the USA's national symbol, and appears on the country's quarter coin and the dollar bill. And if you're lucky enough to witness this remarkable bird in the wild, it's easy to see why.

You can't help but feel inspired and uplifted by this handsome creature as you watch it soar to heights of over 9843ft (3000m). Despite its size – bald eagles weigh in at up to 13lb (6kg) – it circles gracefully in the thermals, its wings spread magnificently across a 6.5ft (2m) span.

Living on the wild side
There is no more thrilling place to see bald eagles than in Alaska's Tongass National Forest. Covering some 26,563 sq miles (68,798 sq km), this temperate rainforest zone is a truly magical place, dripping with old-growth trees, marshes and islands. It's also where the world's largest population of nesting bald eagles resides – around 7000 of them – along with bears, wolves, whales and sea lions that together form a critical part of the ecosystem. Hundreds of songbird species also nest in Tongass' massive, ancient trees, alongside myriad shorebirds and seabirds: you may see Arctic terns, golden-crowned kinglets, marbled murrelets, pigeon guillemots, tufted puffins, Cassin's auklets and more.

Right: A bald eagle at Anan Bear Observatory, Tongass National Forest

Below: Waiting for leftovers in Tongass National Forest

Q&A

Why are bald eagles a big deal?
There was a thriving population of eagles when the American forefathers chose it as the country's symbol, but numbers then declined enormously. These days, eagles bring on a nostalgic idea of the American West and the 'Last Frontier'.

Where does the 'bald' come from?
It's from the Old English word *balde*, meaning white. That said, there were so many older, bald or white-headed senators in the American government when they chose the symbol, people confused the reference: bald heads or white headed!

Something we don't know about bald eagles?
Eagles pair for life but they only stay together if they successfully raise an eaglet. If they don't, the female will abandon the male and she'll find herself a new mate. One famous eagle in Haines has had four partners.

Rachel Cartwright, naturalist

© Ron Niebrugge / Alamy Stock Photo; Chad Graham / Getty Images

Sovereigns of all they survey

Part of the beauty of watching eagles here is hunkering down in one spot for long periods and relaxing in nature. Watching a bald eagle tending to its chicks atop its colossal nest, a platform of large sticks, is mesmerising, generating a true sense of awe in the viewer.

This mighty bird commands deference, presiding over its terrain of shorelines and rivers in the same way a judge does over a court (even its enchanting colouring – a white head and a black 'cloak' – resembles a judge's attire). Its casual glance absorbs the tiniest of detail, its slight movement of head gives nothing away. Then, having eyed another bird's (or even fisher's) catch, it launches itself into the air before swooping in to steal the prey – be it a salmon, herring or flounder – leaving with its prize gripped tenaciously in its talons. This is what prompted US Founding Father Benjamin

Right: A humpback whale diving off Juneau

Far right: Stealing a meal, although there are plenty of salmon to share

Franklin to claim that a bald eagle 'does not get his living honestly'. But it's precisely this skill that creates such amazement.

Remarkably, the soft, high-pitched call of a bald eagle doesn't match its majestic stature: it's as if a sumo wrestler were to sing in counter tenor. It's said that filmmakers used to substitute an eagle's trill with a screech of a hawk to make their scenes more startling. But the bald eagle is one beautiful bird that doesn't need intimidating sounds to be noticed!

Don't Miss

→ **Witnessing a bald eagle shrewdly steal its prey**

→ **Spotting eagles while hiking Tongass' Mendenhall Glacier Meadows Trail**

→ **Heading out on a wildlife-watching boat tour from Juneau**

Find Your Joy

Getting there
The easiest way to reach Tongass National Forest is by air or boat to Juneau – which is itself a good place to spot eagles, via hikes or boat trips.

Accessibility
Juneau has good wheelchair accessibility, and wheelchairs can board the Goldbelt Tram, a five-minute vertical gondola ride to Mt Roberts that offers superb views and where you might be lucky to spot eagles, too. Some boat trips, including whale-watching tours, provide for wheelchairs.

When to go
May to September are the warmest months; depending on the region, salmon runs occur around July, when eagles gather en masse on riverside tree branches to prey on the fish. Avoid the frigid winter (November to April).

Further information
• Free to visitors.
• May to September.
• No specialist facilities.
• There's accommodation and places to eat and drink in Juneau, and cabins and camping in Tongass (fs.usda.gov).
• www.adfg.alaska.gov

© Mariday / Shutterstock; Sergey Uryadnikov / Shutterstock

Other Bald Eagle Hot-spots

Chilkat Valley, Alaska

Each autumn, one of the largest gatherings of bald eagles in the world occurs in the pristine forests of the 75-sq-mile (194-sq-km) Alaska Chilkat Bald Eagle Preserve, on the Chilkat River north of Haines. Attracted by the run of salmon, up to 3000 eagles can gather to joust over fish.

Don't miss

The Alaska Bald Eagle Festival celebrates this phenomenon each November, considered peak eagle gathering time.

Vancouver Island, Canada

Vancouver Island is home to many bald eagles, and you can often see them on wildlife tours, including while whale-watching. From the tour boat, you may be lucky enough to spot two birds engaged in midair courtship, where they lock talons and cartwheel through the air in dramatic fashion.

Don't miss

Heading to the Gulf Islands for excellent chances of spotting eagles and their massive nests, measuring up to 8ft (2.4m) across.

Search for the elusive quetzal in a cloud-forest preserve

 Hiking trails, discovery, wild adventures

 February to June

GUATEMALA

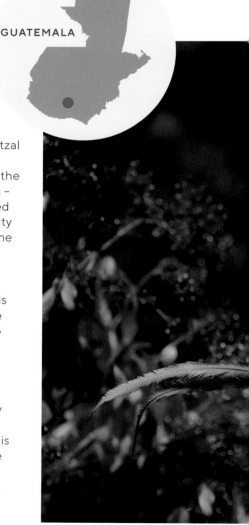

There's a legendary creature hidden away in the dense, mist-covered canopy of Guatemala's cloud forests. With a crimson breast, shimmering blue-green plumage, a spiky emerald crown, sparkling black eyes and 3ft-long (1m), flamboyant twin tail plumes like a carnival dancer, it's considered one of the most beautiful birds in the world. Kings and warriors worshipped it, parents told their children stories about it, and places were named after it. But this iconic creature is no fantasy beast, it's real flesh-and-blood and the national bird of Guatemala: the resplendent quetzal.

A Guatemalan icon

Visitors to Guatemala will spot the quetzal everywhere they go. It's daubed in graffiti, printed on T-shirts, and woven into fabrics. You can buy beaded quetzal keyrings, carved quetzal toys and intricate quetzal jewellery. It even appears on the country's flag and banknotes – Guatemala's currency is called the quetzal, and its second city is called Quetzaltenango – 'the place of the quetzal bird'.

An elusive beauty

Seeing a quetzal in the flesh is much harder, however. These are shy, solitary birds that live high in the remote mountain forests of Central America, such as Guatemala's Mirador Rey Tepepul Preserve. Here the treetops are permanently bathed in damp fog and the bird's vibrant green plumage is well camouflaged against the verdant foliage.

Finding a quetzal requires a healthy helping of fitness and determination. You'll need to

Right: Indigenous Mayan embroidery in Guatemala depicts quetzals

Below: The slightly impractical tail of a quetzal in flight

Q&A

What's so special about the quetzal?
Guatemalans love our national bird. Not only is it exquisite, it represents a connection to our past and hope for the future.

Most interesting thing about them?
Only males have the vivid plumage; females are a more subdued green and brown. It's up to the males to impress the females – the longer his tailfeathers, the more successful he'll be. Then he sheds them at the end of the breeding season and regrows them the next year.

How can I see a quetzal?
You need a guide who knows where the nests are and how to find the birds' favourite feeding spots. And you have to get up before dawn.

But what about my beauty sleep?
The beauty of the quetzal is worth missing a lie-in for.

Alfredo Tol Gonzalez, Birding Atitlán Expeditions guide

© Anton_Ivanov / Shutterstock; Ondrej Prosicky / Shutterstock; Justin Foulkes / Lonely Planet;

Left: Surveying Lake Atitlán and Guatemala's volcanic landscape

Right: A violet sabrewing hummingbird in Monteverde Cloud Forest Biological Reserve

Sacred bird of the Maya

The quetzal wasn't chosen as Guatemala's national bird for its outstanding beauty alone. It's also deeply entwined with the country's history and culture. The Ancient Maya, who dominated Guatemala for over 1000 years, saw the quetzal as a sacred bird. Rulers and priests adorned their headdresses with quetzal tail feathers, and killing one was a crime punishable by death. The legendary Maya warrior hero Tecun Uman is said to have always gone into battle against the Spanish conquistadores accompanied by a spirit guide in the form of a quetzal. When he was fatally wounded near Quetzaltenango in 1524, the bird flew down and embraced him, turning its breast red with his blood.

Today, the Guatemalan people's reverence for the mysterious quetzal gives spotting one an extra frisson of magic that few birding experiences can match.

Don't Miss

→ Watching parent quetzals diving in and out of their nesting holes

→ Spotting toucans, hummingbirds and crested guans in the preserve

→ Enjoying a packed breakfast in the jungle accompanied by the tropical dawn chorus

wake at dawn to trudge up and down slippery mountain trails through the damp undergrowth, ideally accompanied by an experienced guide who can identify the quetzal's high-pitched chirrups, recognise the laurel and wild avocado trees they like to eat from, and spot which rotten tree stumps they've made their nesting holes in.

But it's this challenge that makes the experience even more thrilling – many try to spot a quetzal and fail, so if you do manage to catch a glimpse, you'll know you've earned it.

Find Your Joy

Getting there
From Guatemala City, take a three-hour tourist shuttle to Panajachel, the gateway to Lake Atitlán.

Then hop on a public boat for the 30-minute ride across the lake to Santiago Atitlán, the closest town to Mirador Rey Tepepul. You'll need a guide to visit the preserve: Birding Atitlan (www.atitlanexpeditions. com) offer half-day tours from Santiago Atitlán; bring good walking shoes and a packed breakfast.

Accessibility
Unfortunately, it'll be hard to spot a quetzal if you have mobility challenges. Seeing them involves hiking into the dense jungle; trails can be steep and slippery and there are no bathroom facilities.

When to go
While it's possible to spot quetzals year-round, the best time to see them is during the breeding season, from February to June.

Further information
• No admission fee to the reserve.
• Year-round.
• No specialist facilities.
• Accommodation and restaurants/cafes in Santiago Atitlán.

© Simon Dannhauer / Shutterstock; Kevin Wells Photography / Shutterstock

Other Places to Spot a Quetzal

Monteverde Cloud Forest Biological Reserve, Costa Rica

Covering just over 15 sq miles (40 sq km), mist-shrouded Monteverde in northern Costa Rica is home to 400-plus bird species – including quetzals – as well as around 100 mammal and 490 butterfly species. With well-maintained trails of varying lengths and difficulty, it's relatively accessible and you can hike without a guide – though expert eyes will increase your quetzal-spotting chances.

Don't miss

Taking a night tour to discover roosting birds, nocturnal red-eyed tree frogs and green vine snakes.

Chiriquí Highlands, Panama

Close to the border with Costa Rica, the Chiriquí Highlands enjoy the cool and humid forest environment that quetzals love. The area's main town, Boquete, sits in the shadow of Panama's tallest mountain, Volcán Barú, surrounded by a spiderweb of hiking trails through the tropical jungle.

Don't miss

Walking through the treetops on the Hanging Bridges Tour for the chance of an eye-level quetzal encounter.

Meet the stalkers of the swamps in Buenos Aires

♡ Urban nature, diverse species, waterfront trails

🕐 September to November

ARGENTINA

The noise of downtown Buenos Aires begins to recede as you cross the Río Dársena Sur. A few short blocks later, birds start to appear: monk parakeets perch on the railing alongside Laguna de los Coipos, where ringed teals and other ducks swim. Inside the Reserva Ecológica Costanera Sur, long-legged wattled jacanas stride across the wetlands, their colouring dramatically split between black heads and necks and rust-red back and tailfeathers.

Herons and egrets, too, stalk the lagoons in search of food, as do aquatic rodents called nutria – coipo in Spanish – their whiskered noses lifted as they swim in search of tasty plants. Nearby, a mourning dove on a tree stump intermittently utters its soft coo: whoo-HOO-hoo-hoo. The

soothing call, the focused feeding of the waterbirds and the flap and flutter of various other wings are particularly captivating, given the proximity of the city centre.

From rubble to reserve

This urban oasis, now a paradise for over 300 bird species, didn't start out as a natural wetland: it was the byproduct of land-creation works for a new administrative district, in which rubble was dumped into the Río de la Plata. After the plans were shelved in 1984, nature took over. The site was colonised by plants, birds and other wildlife, and several conservation organisations joined together to propose the creation of an ecological reserve here. In 1986, the 865-acre (350-hectare) Reserva Ecológica Costanera Sur was inaugurated by the city government.

Right: Great egrets are abundant in Buenos Aires' wetlands

Below: The Reserva Ecológica Costanera Sur is on the edge of the city

© LMPark Photos / Shutterstock; Cavan-Images / Shutterstock; Francis Philippe / Shutterstock; vergie azevedo / Shutterstock

Q&A

What's unique about this reserve?
Many tourists can't believe there's a reserve with a lot of impressive birds so close to the city centre.

When's the best time to visit?
Early morning and late afternoon are typically when birds are most active, but birds of prey come out when the sun has risen, so to see them it's better closer to noon. October has the most species, but there are birds we only see in winter. There is always a time and place to see birds.

Any advice for visitors?
Look in all directions. As you are walking, look ahead and see what comes your way. Raise your head and look up. Look down, because some birds walk on the edges of the lagoons or in the gutters alongside the roads. Be patient, because this is like going fishing.

Simón Tagtachian, Costanera Sur Birdwatchers Club coordinator

Over the years, more species found a home at Costanera Sur, and in 2005 it was recognised internationally as a Ramsar Site (a wetland of international importance) and an Area of Importance for the Conservation of Birds.

Now, as you walk through the reserve, it feels like these lagoons and marshes must always have been here. It seems impossible that one of South America's largest cities could be just a short walk away – until you raise your eyes to the high-rise buildings towering on the not-so-distant horizon. Turn around, though, and the vastness of the Río de la Plata delta looks like the open sea, with no hint of the distant opposite shore.

Space to breathe

Birdwatchers aren't the only ones who flock to this slice of urban paradise. Cyclists and runners love the 5.5 miles (8.8 km) of flat, lightly gravelled trails, and families

Right: A Brazilian guinea pig in the Reserva Ecológica Costanera Sur

Far right: The forest surrounding Iguazú Falls is an important habitat

come here for recreation and waterfront picnics. But it's the birds that are at the heart of the reserve, with nearly 150 year-round residents, and many other seasonal species and migrants present during different months.

A place that began as a dumping site for construction debris has evolved into arguably the most important green space in Buenos Aires. As a Harris's hawk circles overhead or a rufous-bellied thrush trills its melodic song, the huge metropolis just a short walk away feels distant indeed.

Don't Miss

→ Watching wattled jacanas and other waders in the wetlands

→ Spotting raptors in flight, looking for prey

→ Listening to birdsong in the heart of the city as the day ends

Find Your Joy

Getting there
Reserva Ecológica Costanera Sur is located directly opposite downtown Buenos Aires,
less than a mile (1.6km) from the city's main square, Plaza de Mayo. There are entrances at the northwest and southwest corners of the reserve. Several downtown metro stations and bus stops are within a 20-minute walk.

Accessibility
Trails through the reserve's habitats are
generally flat and lightly gravelled, making them suitable for wheelchairs and strollers.

When to go
September to November for the greatest variety of birds, but there are typically well over 100 species present at any time of year.

Further information
• Free to visitors.
• Open year-round.
• Visitor centre at southwest entrance.
• Cafes and restaurants within easy walking distance.
• Hotels nearby in central Buenos Aires.
• www. reservacostanera. com.ar

© Carolina Jaramillo / Shutterstock; Matt Munro, Lonely Planet

Other Argentine Birding Locations

Iguazú Falls, Misiones Province

Spanning the border between Argentina and Brazil, these spectacular falls are surrounded by lush rainforest that's home to over 400 bird species, as well as coatis, monkeys, jaguars, jaguarundis, ocelots and more. On the Argentine side, many birds can be seen along the trails through the rainforest close to the falls. The less-visited Macuco Trail offers a higher probability of spotting rarer species.

Don't miss
Spotting toucans in the fruit trees.

Iberá Wetlands, Corrientes Province

It takes effort to reach this huge expanse of marsh, swamp and lagoons in northeastern Argentina, but the reward is excellent opportunities to spot some of Iberá's 400-plus bird species, as well as capybaras, giant otters, armadillos, caimans and monkeys. Visit between March and May for comfortable temperatures and abundant birdlife, or during the somewhat rainier but vibrant September-to-November breeding season.

Don't miss
Seeing South America's largest bird, the greater rhea.

Spot the birds that inspired Darwin's theories of natural selection

 Remote islands, scientific relevance, varied songs

 January and February, nesting time for finches

ECUADOR

If there were a theatre for birdwatching, to rival Italy's La Scala, it would be the Galápagos, a legendary volcanic archipelago comprising 19 islands and scattered islets off the coast of Ecuador.

Here, birds take centre stage in glorious surroundings – along with non-feathered costars, from sea lions to land iguanas. Few other places on Earth are more suited to experiencing birdlife as this remarkable region – where bird calls echo off cliffs, where chirps escape from thorny thickets, where shrills emanate from the skies. Hearing the vocals of a Galápagos mockingbird or the beak-clapping of a waved albatross in this extraordinary and remote location will likely make you a birdwatcher forever.

Watching from the wings
While binoculars, like opera glasses, will help you focus on the plumage and bright-blue feet of the blue-footed booby, or on the vivid red pouch of the magnificent frigate bird, inflating as it courts its partner, the naked eye is all you really need to see birds here. And this is mind-blowing: many animals and birds are not afraid of you entering their territory. Stay still, breathe quietly, move slowly... and wait for the magic to happen. It doesn't get better than being able to view an avian performance from the (stage) wings.

Small compared to fellow Galápagos stars like the flamingo (known for its orange-pink fluffy 'skirt') and the lava gull (a rare sighting, famed for its extraordinary leg-stretching routines), one modest bird deserves extra attention. Enter Darwin's finches, of which the 13 surviving species are endemic to the islands.

Right: A blue-footed booby on North Seymour Island

Below: The beaks of Darwin's finches offer an insight into the theory of evolution

Q&A

The Galápagos: 'too far, too expensive!' Agree?
This is a special place – it's worth the trip and the experience. I've been in other amazing places with amazing birds and marine ecosystems but this is unique. It's the Galápagos!

What Galápagos birding experience shouldn't I miss?
Head off in boats to tick off sightings of pelagic birds, such as the waved albatross, northern storm petrel and Audubon's shearwater. And visit the different islands to observe the differences between the finches.

Birds or other animals – which wins?
You are putting me in an awkward position – it's the Galápagos! Even though I usually give birds preference, the Galápagos is very different. It's everything – the sum of its parts. I'm also an ecologist and I love the marine environment; some of the most special things are under the water.

Jorge Maldonado, ornithologist & ecologist

© Ryan M. Bolton / Shutterstock; Tristan Brown / Getty Images; Steve Allen / Shutterstock

Left: A common cactus finch on South Plaza Island

Right: A frigate bird flashes his throat pouch on North Seymour Island

Don't Miss

→ **Staying still and letting the wildlife come to you**

→ **Watching Darwin's finches flitting from twig to branch**

→ **Spotting the vivid vermillion flycatcher**

With a keen eye, you might spot woodpecker and mangrove finches, plus two species of warbler-finch (green and grey), three of tree finch (small, medium and large), four of ground finch (the sharp-beaked, and the small, medium and large), and the common and large cactus finch.

Darwin's starlets

Nothing will prepare you for observing these finches in the wild, but not because of their outlandish behaviour (skittish), their colours (some muted; others more vibrant) or their melodic chirping. Measuring between 4in and 8in (10cm to 20cm), these tiny creatures get top billing for their huge effect on the human world.

These very songbirds influenced Darwin's theories of natural selection, thanks to their different beaks, and evolved to adapt to different conditions and different types of food. For any viewer – from experienced twitcher to first-time birder – understanding that significance as you watch the ancestors of the finches Darwin observed is mind-boggling.

OK, we concede that some scientists and ornithologists are now claiming that finches may have had less effect on Darwin's theories than previously thought. But this doesn't lessen the thrill of seeing them in their natural habitat; and if these feathery icons have lost their star billing, they are none the wiser. Seeing them is to understand the world; these treasures are a joy to behold.

Find Your Joy

Getting there
The only way to get to the Galápagos is by air from mainland Ecuador. There are airports on Baltra and San Cristóbal. Flights are often arranged in conjunction with a cruise. Independent travellers can book boat excursions and guides in main hub towns, such as Puerto Ayora on Santa Cruz.

Accessibility
Puerto Ayora is reasonably accessible. Other islands are remote, with unavoidable pathways of dirt or rock. That said, some Galápagos travel companies do cater to wheelchair users and people with limited mobility; ask ahead.

When to go
The Galápagos can be visited year-round. Each month brings its own weather conditions, rewards, sightings and animal behaviour.

Further information
• Admission charge for Galápagos National Park.
• Year-round.
• No specialist facilities, expert guides available.
• Accommodation and refreshments in the main villages of Santa Cruz, San Cristóbal, Isabela and Floreana.
• www.galapagos. gob.ec

© Stubblefield Photography / Shutterstock; SigWorld / Shutterstock

Other Galápagos Birding Sites

Red-footed booby, San Cristóbal and Genovesa islands

With distinct, vivid-red legs, the photogenic red-footed booby is a Galápagos favourite. Although clumsy on land, it's a deft flier, diving into the ocean from heights to catch prey, usually small fish. It often gathers and nests in colonies, and both male and female incubate the eggs.

Don't miss
Spotting the fluffy heads of chicks as they peer from nests in low-lying trees or bushes.

Magnificent frigatebird, North Seymour Island

Best known for its bright red throat pouch, the aptly named magnificent frigatebird has the largest wingspan – over 6.5ft (2m) – to body-weight ratio of any bird in the world. It also has a unique courting ritual: to attract a female, the male inflates his throat pouch while beating his bill rapidly on this 'balloon'.

Don't miss
Mating season, when colonies such as that on North Seymour are as noisy as a drumming circle.

Swing through the suburbs in search of burrowing owls

 Drive-by birding, spotting owlets, surprising sightings

 January to June

USA

Some birding experiences require a jungle trek or an excursion to a remote island, but in Cape Coral – the largest city between Tampa and Miami – it's as easy as cruising suburban streets with your windows rolled down (or your walking shoes laced up) and your eyes at ground level. This Gulf Coast town is home to Florida's largest population of burrowing owls, drawn here in the 1950s when developers began clearing trees for a planned community, leaving behind the abundant open spaces that they need to thrive.

Standing about as tall and wide as a large iced coffee, burrowing owls are masters of adaptability, with a range that extends from western Canada all the way down to Tierra del Fuego at the tip of South America. And in some parts of this range, it might be more accurate to call them 'borrowing' owls, since they've been known to commandeer tunnels dug by prairie dogs or gopher tortoises.

Owls, owls, everywhere...
During a 2022 count, over 1700 adults and 2000 juveniles were recorded in Cape Coral, and they're everywhere: in parks, behind the public library, on little-league fields and golf courses, or simply sitting on front lawns like attentive garden gnomes. To find them, just look for the PVC pipes that the city uses to mark off burrows and keep mowers at bay.

Right: Most burrowing owls borrow burrows dug by other creatures

Below: Suburban Cape Coral, prime burrowing owl real estate

Q&A

Any quirky spots where you've encountered burrowing owls?
We've found their burrows near and under signs, fire hydrants, median strips and storm drains. We often find them sitting on windowsills – some residents say they are being watched by the owls.

How can residents protect them?
Drive slower. Don't use pesticides or herbicides near burrows. And put a starter burrow in your yard! Habitat is being lost by hundreds of burrows a year due to new construction.

What do you love about the owls?
My husband and I have rescued many burrowing owls, and they have personalities. We returned one back to his nest and as he approached his burrow, his buddy came out. We were concerned, but immediately they snuggled up to each other, and it was almost like one put his wing over the other. We cried – it was so heartwarming.

Judy Mitchell, Cape Coral Friends of Wildlife president

© Tathoms / Shutterstock; Nadezda Murmakova / Shutterstock; Don Mammoser / Shutterstock; Jim Schwabel / Shutterstock

Unlike with some owls, you don't need to head out after dark to snag a sighting. Burrowing owls are active during the day, and are often seen standing on their long legs at burrow entrances, surveying the landscape like a nosy neighbour.

Their bright yellow eyes are exceedingly expressive, making it tempting to anthropomorphise them. Their wide eyes seem to signify shock, a squint of the brow might convey suspicion, a 90-degree head-tilt looks as if they're clowning around. We read those facial cues as pure personality and can't help but fall for them.

Right: Monogamous monk parakeets in Cape Coral

Far right: A sharp-witted scrub jay in Oscar Scherer State Park

Reasons to celebrate

While they may seem abundant here, burrowing owls are fast losing habitats and are listed as a threatened species in Florida. Luckily, they have cheerleaders in their corner. Cape Coral Friends of Wildlife volunteers help repair and clean existing burrows, stake and map new ones, teach residents how to collect owlets on rainy days to prevent drowning, and offer tips on digging your own starter burrow.

Come February, at the beginning of nesting season, Cape Coral honours its official city bird with a Burrowing Owl Festival at Rotary Park, complete with speeches, vendors and a bus tour. If you're lucky, you may meet one of the city's fluffy new owlet residents and perhaps hear its unique sonic adaptation: a raspy hiss of a warning call that sounds exactly like a rattlesnake.

Don't Miss

→ Spotting fluffy owl chicks in the spring

→ Listening for the owls' unique vocalisations, from coo-cooing to snake-like hissing

→ Scanning telephone wires for the area's feral (but charming!) monk parakeets

Find Your Joy

Getting there
Cape Coral is about a half-hour drive from Southwest Florida International Airport in neighbouring Fort Myers. Once you drive into Cape Coral, keep your eyes peeled, as owls can be seen quite literally anywhere around the city.

Accessibility
Because this is a great place to birdwatch from behind the wheel or on the sidewalk, it's ideal for birders of all mobility levels.

When to go
January to June is the ideal time to see burrowing owls in Florida, as the moderate weather means they aren't hiding underground from the heat; owlets start emerging from burrows around April.

Further information
• Free to visitors.
• Year-round.
• No specialist facilities.
• Accommodation, restaurants and bars in Cape Coral.
• www. ccfriendsofwildlife.org

© Frank Fichtmueller / Shutterstock; Donna Bollenbach / Shutterstock

Other Suburban Florida Hot-spots

Oscar Scherer State Park

This park near Sarasota may look unassuming, but its sandy, scrubby landscape is the perfect habitat for the state's only endemic bird species, the Florida scrub-jay. On the 15 miles (24km) of trails, hikers and bikers often spot these charismatic birds as they cache acorns for later safekeeping.

Don't miss

Snapping a selfie with the super-curious jays, which sometimes land on birders' backpacks or heads.

Fort De Soto Park

Set across five interconnected keys just outside St Petersburg, the 1136-acre (460-hectare) park is known for its sandy beaches and military fortifications from the Spanish–American War. Thanks to its prime location on the migratory flight path from Canada, it's a popular stopover point in the spring and autumn, attracting more than 325 species over the years.

Don't miss

Watching various species of tiny plovers as they dart around in the surf.

Soak up canyon-side views of soaring Andean condors

♡ Sacred birds, epic outlooks, shifting landscapes

🕐 March to June

I n the vastness of Cañón del Colca in southern Peru, Andean condors soar and pivot with lyrical, graceful swoops. For the Inca, these huge birds were heavenly messengers, unique and rarefied creatures whose endurance and speed enabled them to ferry humans from this life to the next. Standing at the canyon's rim, as condors glide and float within a few feet of onlookers' heads, these magnificent 'sky guardians' often evoke a sense of utter wonder and smallness in anyone lucky enough to witness them.

Aerial bliss above the abyss

En route to Cañón del Colca from nearby Arequipa, you'll cut through the precipitous Paso de Patopampa, perhaps pausing for a steaming cup of coca tea at 16,110ft (4910m) above sea level. But the superlative statistics don't end once you reach your destination: Colca is one of the deepest canyons on the planet, plunging down some 13,650ft (4160m) – twice the depth of the Grand Canyon. Included in Green Destinations' 2020 Global Top 100 list for its sustainable tourism initiatives, this wild wonderland of shifting landscapes is also Peru's top spot in which to see condors in all their untamed glory. Cañón del Colca's thin maw provides the ideal plunging playground for these giant birds, whose wingspans can stretch up to 11ft (3.3m). They live here

Right: An Andean condor in the Colca Canyon, with sightseers for scale

Below: Andean condors ride the thermals from the base of the deep Colca Canyon

Q&A

Why is Cañón del Colca special?
It's the best place in the world to observe condors, a magical and religious symbol for the cultures of the Indigenous Colca people.

Best time to spot condors?
Condors live here all the time. There is erroneous information for tourists, such as 'go in the morning because they appear at 8am, disappear at 9am', and that's it. Wrong. The condor lives there. It feeds its chick, returns to the nest constantly, and comes back until sunset.

How long should you spend here?
You should stay in the canyon for at least two days to see everything.

Any advice for first-time visitors?
Bring walking sticks. Some of the trails aren't well-marked, and GPS will not help you. I don't recommend going alone.

Vlado Soto, Colca Trek/Colca Trek Lodge owner & guide

© Eric Isselee / Shutterstock; rbulthuis / Getty Images; Cezary Wojtkowski / Shutterstock; Galyna Andrushko / Shutterstock

Left: Reaching the Colca Canyon requires some trekking

Right: The Uros people create reed islands and boats to float on Lake Titicaca

before seeing the deep-brown outlines of condors descending delicately into your line of vision. Eventually, they come so close that you can make out the details of each feather before a gust of wind elevates them back up toward the canyon lip.

Adventurous souls can explore the Cañón del Colca's depths on a guided hike, zigzagging down a network of dirt trails to the very bottom, where there are plenty of opportunities to set up camp and soak in the hot springs. The trek from rim to floor takes two to three days – at night, you'll be rewarded with an inky, star-splattered sky devoid of artificial light; the days bring plenty of new vantage points to view condors' graceful glides.

Peru's unofficial second national anthem, 'El Cóndor Pasa', pays homage to these iconic birds. But nothing compares to being in the natural sanctuary of Cañón del Colca and seeing them with your own eyes.

Don't Miss

→ Watching the silent swoop and surge of condors from the mirador

→ Soaking in steaming springs after hiking to the canyon floor

→ Gazing into the narrow abyss from the canyon's lip

year-round, shielding their chicks in precipitous canyon-side nests. While the young stay snug high above, adult condors take flight into the sheer-walled canyon in majestic, silent swoops, riding the air currents as they scan for prey below.

Among the canyon guardians
Mirador Cruz del Cóndor is the best place to pay your respects to these dignified sky-lords. Sit or stand quietly on the rocky outlook, where the canyon views span to the horizon, and you'll only have to wait a few minutes

Find Your Joy

Getting there
Cañón del Colca is easily visited from nearby Arequipa. Take a bus from Terrapuerto de

Arequipa bus station to Cabanaconde (around 4½ hours), then a 20-minute taxi ride to Mirador Cruz del Cóndor; or rent a car in Arequipa and drive the winding mountain roads to the mirador yourself. Book guided canyon hikes in town: try Colca Trek (www.colcatrek.com.pe).

Accessibility
Trekking into the canyon

itself will be challenging for those with limited mobility, but trails around the rim are relatively flat, and the mirador is accessible by road.

When to go
Colca's condors can be seen year-round, but are most active during the dry season months (March to June), when the trails are generally in

better condition, too.

Further information
• Admission charge.
• Open year-round.
• No specialist facilities.
• Restaurants in nearby Chivay.
• Accommodation in Pinchollo, Yanque and Cabanaconde.
• www.colcaperu.gob.pe

© Lukas Uher / Shutterstock; Philip Lee Harvey / Lonely Planet

Other Peruvian Birding Highlights

Lake Titicaca

At 12,507ft (3812m) above sea level, Titicaca is home to some of the region's most astounding wetland birds, including the Puna ibis, yellow-shouldered blackbird and Titicaca flightless grebe. Venture out onto the lake's glassy, chilly waters and you're bound to come face-to-beak with these elusive creatures.

Don't miss

Boating to the floating Islas Uros to see unique, reed-based isles teeming with birds like the Andean goose and black-faced ibis.

Cuzco

Cuzco's prime location in the Sacred Valley makes it an ideal base for seeing all manner of jewel-toned hummingbirds – which, like condors, were heralded by the Inca as tiny messengers of the gods. Species such as the Tyrian metaltail and the sparkling violetear soar, flutter and nest throughout Cuzco and the surrounding areas.

Don't miss

Taking a day trip to Ensifera Camp, a hummingbird sanctuary where you can spot up to 18 species on tours or self-guided walks.

Behold thundering snow geese flocks on the BC Bird Trail

 Migratory visitors, endemic species, urban trails

 March to April & October to December

CANADA

To the south of Vancouver and its dense forest of skyscrapers, it is raining – fat drops, hard and heavy. The ground is momentarily deluged, the distant backdrop of the North Shore Mountains covered in a thin film of white cloud. The surface of the Fraser River seems to tremble from the downpour and the water flows on, past the aptly-named city of Delta then out from the marshland into the Strait of Georgia.

The air takes on an earthy smell – and in the middle of the scene is a congregation of positively cheery snow geese, honking as if having the best day of their lives. This is no ordinary huddle of native American waterfowl, however. There are some 10,000 of them, making it one of the world's largest gatherings of migratory birds – and ensemble trumpeting is guaranteed.

Islands in the stream

The story of the snow geese is of two different realities, some 3000 miles (4800km) apart. From May to August, these pink-billed highfliers breed amid the melting snows, thawing ice and tundra foraging-grounds of northern Alaska, the Canadian Arctic and Wrangel Island off northern Russia. They then fly south in sky-crowding flocks to savour the warmer northern-hemisphere winters in Mexico's Gulf Coastal Plain and the southern US.

The real winners during this mass exodus are birders in British Columbia, with binoculars and cameras and empty diaries. The waterfowl have become part of the autumn calendar at BC Bird Trail sites south of Vancouver, where the viridescent wetlands inland of Boundary Bay's north shore are a favourite scheduled

Right: Snow geese pairs partner-up for life

Below: Snow geese gather with Vancouver's North Shore mountains in the distance

Q&A

What's it like to see the migration?
Seeing the fields turn snow-white with huge flocks of snow geese is spectacular – and the cacophony of sounds can be equally impressive.

What else can you see and hear?
We see huge numbers of migratory shorebirds stopping over to feed on vast mudflats, and diverse species of songbirds such as warblers. Their dawn chorus in the spring and summer is amazing. Occasionally during migration season, we even experience something called a 'fallout', when hundreds of birds 'fall out' of their migration into an unlikely habitat area like Queen Elizabeth Park in Vancouver, in response to certain weather conditions. Trees can literally drip with hundreds of beautiful warblers.

What other tips would you share?
Plan your visit in advance; reservations are required to visit the George C Reifel, for instance.

Liron Gertsman, BC birding guide

© haseg77 / Shutterstock; Feng Yu / Shutterstock

stop on the Pacific Flyway –
the north-to-south migratory
route that extends down
to Patagonia. And on these
estuarine wetlands, the comfort
the waterfowl take from
refuelling and resting every year
is palpable.

Tracing ancestral patterns
BC Bird Trail highlights include
the South Fraser Bird Trail, with
a number of beautiful birding
locations on the traditional
territories of the Tsawwassen,
Musqueam and other Coast
Salish First Nation peoples.
Eagles and ospreys gather at
Iona Beach Regional Park; in
nearby Richmond, the 3.7-mile
(6km) West Dyke Trail unfolds
between wildflowers and sea-to-
summit views from Terra Nova
Rural Park to Garry Point Park in
the company of hawks, herons
and owls.
  The high-flying army of
geese also takes up temporary
residence at George C Reifel

Right: The
George C Reifel
Bird Sanctuary
in the Alaksen
National Wildlife

Far right: Beach
huts offer shelter
on Skanör beach
at Falsterbo,
Sweden

Migratory Bird Sanctuary, just
south on Westham Island.
Its observation tower is the
pinnacle of one of Canada's
most terrific birdwatching sites.
Other species, such as black-
bellied plover, dunlin, black-
capped chickadee and western
sandpiper, patrol the tideline
as traditional custodians of the
land, but the ultimate revelatory
thrill here is the sight of skeins of
snow geese almost blacking out
the sky, or filling an entire field
with rowdy noise and dance as if
attending a rock-music festival.

Don't Miss

→ **Craning your neck to
watch 10,000-plus geese
take flight**

→ **Discovering 300
resident and migratory
species at George C Reifel
Sanctuary**

→ **Joining the songbirds
on the bike-friendly West
Dyke Trail**

Find Your Joy

Getting there
Fly to Vancouver, then
hire a car or take a
Translink bus or train
(www.translink.ca) south

to Delta and Richmond.
There is no public transit
from these gateway
towns to the bird-
thronged coastline and
estuary sites of the BC
Bird Trail, so you'll need
to drive or take a taxi.

Accessibility
British Columbia's cities
are well geared up for
travellers with limited
mobility. Like other BC

Bird Trail sites, the South
Fraser and West Dyke
Trails, and the George C
Reifel Sanctuary, have
wheelchair-accessible
boardwalk trails.

When to go
There are two periods
where you're guaranteed
to see the snow geese:
from March to April,
and from October to
December.

Further information
• Fee for George C
Reifel Sanctuary (book
in advance); BC Bird
Trail sites are free.
• Year-round.
• Hides available.
• Accommodation and
restaurants in Delta
and Richmond.
• www.bcbirdtrail.ca

Falsterbo, Sweden

Sometimes, what turns birders' heads is just the sheer numbers – and at the Falsterbo Peninsula, jutting into the Øresund Strait in southwest Sweden, some 500 million migratory birds stop to rest and refuel every September and October. Species seen here include barn swallows, western yellow wagtails, common eiders, bramblings and blue tits, as well as huge gatherings of raptors.

Don't miss

Scanning the skies for sparrowhawks, marsh harriers and European honey buzzards.

Handa Island, Scotland

With precipitous Torridonian sandstone cliffs and waves that pulsate with orchestral intensity below, this nature reserve, offshore of Sutherland in the northwest Highlands, is a grand setting for the 100,000-odd seabirds that flit in every year. There are razorbills and great skuas diving into the rich feeding grounds of the Atlantic, and unrivalled opportunities to watch one of the British Isles' largest guillemot colonies at play.

Don't miss

Seeing puffins in their hundreds from May to July.

© Max Lindenthaler / Shutterstock

Meet the (avian) ancestors on a hummingbird-spotting hike

COLOMBIA

 Spirituality, connection with nature, Indigenous history

 December to March

In Colombia's Laguna de Guatavita nature reserve, every birding hike starts the same. Indigenous Muisca guides ask for a blessing from Pacha Mama (Mother Earth) – a request for safety on the trail, and guidance in the face of dangers. Crucially, they ask permission: the Earth is the authority, the hikers only visitors. Nature's response might be good weather or easy terrain – but there is one sign that supersedes all others, one messenger acting as a quivering ambassador: the hummingbird.

These tiny, jewel-like birds, which flit around nectar-rich flowers here in their thousands, are embedded in pre-Columbian spiritualism, seen as ancestors reincarnated. The Muisca believe that a close encounter with a hummingbird is a way to commune with their forbearers, to receive messages from their progenitors and from the landscape itself.

Shattered landscapes reborn

Here in Colombia's central highlands, a tumultuous history ties the Indigenous people to their earthly inheritance. After Spanish conquistadors witnessed the Muisca king draped in painted gold during a sacred ritual at Laguna de Guatavita, their fever dream of finding the mythical El Dorado engendered centuries of unspeakable colonial violence. They enslaved the Muisca in 1625 and set them to the painstaking, decades-long task of draining the lake and chipping away at the surrounding ridge in search of riches. Like a ceramic bowl cleanly fractured on the kitchen floor, the lagoon basin today has a chunk cleaved from its side.

But an El Dorado, of sorts, can be found here. Inspired by their

Right: Pre-Columbian gold antiquities in Bogotá's Museo de Oro

Below: A sparkling violetear hummingbird, found in Colombia's highlands

My Birding Joy

Under dappled forest shadow, we're gathered, heads bent. Before beginning our ascent towards the rim of the Laguna Guatavita we're led in prayer by Paula, a Muisca guide working in conservation. It's as though I'm back listening to grace around a family table, unsure of the correct words but determined to show respect.

But as Paula is reciting the benediction 'thank you for the ground we walk on', she lets out a cry. Our heads snap up, alarmed. Paula watches a forest-green sword-billed hummingbird flutter close to our heads. She beams, speaking softly in Muisca to her ancestral emissary. 'You know, they didn't really take our gold,' she exclaims, as she watches the tiny bird dart into the trees. 'This is our gold. Our gold is green.'

SJ Armstrong

© Artush / Shutterstock; Bruno M Photographie / Shutterstock; Milan Zygmunt / Shutterstock

Left: Laguna de Guatavita, source of many Muisca myths

Right: A Tolima blossomcrown hummingbird feeds from flowers

Don't Miss

→ Scanning lagoon-side farmlands for iridescent indigo-capped hummers

→ Watching condors soar over the mountains from Guatavita's lakeside trails

→ Admiring the Andes' unique plant life, from tufted frailejóns to blooming brugmansia

ancestors and their connection to the land, the Muisca have led enormous efforts to revitalise the landscape of Laguna de Guatavita. The local authority has collaborated closely with them to limit visitors to the reserve, eliminate plastics and other waste and reintroduce and nourish native plants that were supplanted by gold-rushing greed. Once again able to supp at the stems of pink and crimson flowers, the hundreds of hummingbird species native to the Colombian Andes have returned to commune with the inheritors of this storied land.

Resurrecting gods

Today, the return of the wildlife and the resurrection of the plant life are a testament to the work of Guatavita's Indigenous caretakers. Every bird sighting speaks to the recovery. Every quiver of a purple wing or sharp dart of an emerald-green bodice sparks joy. Every trembling sip of nectar from flowers draped over the trees tells a tale of revitalisation and resilience. Though they range from technicolour dazzlers, such as the turquoise-headed sparkling violetear to more muted members of the family, like the white-bellied woodstar, hummingbirds are easily defined by their characteristic cutlass beaks and standstill flight.

Though far from the golden trinkets that once drew conquistadors to Guatavita, the natural treasures that attract travellers today still glimmer like jewels in Colombia's sun.

Find Your Joy

Getting there
Bogotá's El Dorado International Airport is around 35 miles (56km) southwest of Laguna de

Guatavita. Get to the reserve via a 40-minute taxi ride from the nearby town of Guatavita, or take a Sesquilé-bound bus from Bogotá's north terminal and ask to stop off there en route. A guide is mandatory within Laguna de Guatavita – try Native Birding Colombia (www.nativebirdingcolombia.com). Plastic bottles are banned in the reserve and

are confiscated on entry.

Accessibility
As the reserve's trails are uneven and sometimes steep, they're not accessible to wheelchair users, or travellers with limited mobility.

When to go
While the weather remains temperate year-round, the dry season (December

to March) offers the best bird-spotting opportunities.

Further information
• Admission charge.
• Open year-round.
• No specialist facilities.
• Shop at the entrance.
• Accommodation and restaurants in Guatavita town.
• www.colparques.net/lguatavita

© Heinner / Shutterstock; Andrew M Allport / Shutterstock

Other Colombian Birding Excursions

High Andes, Tolima

West of Bogotá, the great green hills, towering palms and coffee plantations of the Andean volcanic belt are home to over 1000 bird species. On an Indigenous-led tour with Aweima Birding, explore the unique paramo ecosystem and look for endemic birds like the Tolima dove, Cauca guan or Tolima blossomcrown hummingbird, as well as colourful purple-backed thornbill hummingbirds, golden-headed quetzals and rainbow-bearded thornbills.

Don't miss
Meeting the vivid gaze of the Stygian owl.

Mitú-Vaupés, Amazonía

Some 1300 species of birds are native to the Amazon Basin, and at Mitú-Vaupés, in southeastern Colombia, you can get an insiders' perspective on spotting the most elusive species with a guide from the Tucano people. Birding tours might deliver sightings of toucans teetering in the treetops, vast swarms of parakeets migrating at sunset or the tangerine mohawk of the Guianan cock-of-the-rock.

Don't miss
The topaz, chestnut or bespeckled bellies of Amazonía's many antbird species.

Observe iconic American birds in Boston's garden cemetery

 Serenity, history, urban escape

 Year-round

USA

Passing through the gates of Mt Auburn is like stepping into a peaceful world, far removed from the busy urban streets beyond. No surprise there, perhaps – after all, it is a cemetery – but perhaps more striking is how lush and lovely the place is. In spring, the many trees and flowers burst into bloom; in summer the grounds are richly green. Come autumn, the changing leaves bring vibrant colour to contrast with the grey headstones. Winter has its own beauty, especially when snow cloaks the rolling terrain.

And all year round there are birds. Ever-present robins, flitting across the ground and perching on headstones; bold blue jays pecking energetically at seeds while a red-tailed hawk fixes alert eyes on potential prey. Here, bright red flashes as a cardinal flits from tree to tree; there, brilliant yellow as a goldfinch trills and twitters on a branch. As if in answer, a black-capped chickadee emits the distinctive call – chick-a-dee-dee-dee – that gives it its name.

Wild turkeys stride between graves, while at Willow Pond, a great blue heron wades in the shallows, nabbing fish with quick dips of its beak. On the opposite shore, painted turtles bask in the sunshine, slipping smoothly into the water when startled. Mt Auburn may be a place of final rest, but it's equally full of life.

A different kind of cemetery
The idea of a cemetery as a beautiful, tranquil place designed to both honour

Right: A wild turkey in Brookline, just outside Boston

Below: An American robin contemplates mortality in a Boston cemetery

Q&A

What makes Mt Auburn special?
It's an oasis of green in an urban area and therefore a welcome stop for migratory birds to rest and refuel. The diverse horticultural collections and natural features attract both migrants and year-round residents.

Do you have a favourite season?
Late winter to early spring is a wonderful time, before the crowds of birders show up. There are still the winter resident birds, but also some early harbingers of spring. The best part is there are no leaves on the trees yet, so the birds are easy to spot.

Any crowd favourites?
The resident red-tailed hawks always delight visitors. They're large enough to see without binoculars and are often spotted perched artfully atop monuments.

What's your number-one tip?
Check the crowd-sourced 'Bird Sightings' board at the front gate for recent reports of birds and locations.

Jessica Bussmann, Mt Auburn director of education & visitor services

© Charles Brutlag / Shutterstock; Micha Weber / Shutterstock; DesignTop / Shutterstock; Birchmarine / Shutterstock

© Gean Sabin / Shutterstock; Wisan-kun Jie / Shutterstock

the dead and inspire the living through nature and art was revolutionary when Mt Auburn was established in 1831. The different sections of the cemetery reflect nearly two centuries of landscape architecture, burial traditions and memorial art, a rich heritage that has earned Mt Auburn the designation of National Historic Landmark.

In between watching the many-coloured birds, check out the graves of prominent Americans buried here, including – to name just a few – artist Winslow Homer, author Bernard Malamud, architect Charles Bulfinch, reformer Dorothea Dix and poet Henry Wadsworth Longfellow.

Right: The iconic northern cardinal is the state bird of seven US states

Far right: An aerial view of Halibut Point State Park, north of Boston

Migrants & residents

Mt Auburn is particularly renowned as a birdwatching destination during the spring migration, which takes places roughly between mid-April and mid-May. During the peak migration it's possible to see as many as 100 bird species in the cemetery. Come in the early morning, and chances are you'll be treated to a chorus of birdsong from dozens of different species of warblers.

However, while the migration is famous, there are excellent reasons to visit in any season. Many classic American birds are present throughout much or all of the year; others come and go. The beauty of Mt Auburn is that no matter what month it is, there's plenty of wonderful winged life to be seen amid the testaments to human lives once lived.

Don't Miss

➜ **Basking in the sounds of the cemetery's abundant songbirds**

➜ **Climbing the Washington Tower for a bird's-eye view of Boston**

➜ **Looking for raptors perched in trees above the graves**

Find Your Joy

Getting there
Located in Cambridge, just across the Charles River from central Boston, the cemetery is reachable from Harvard Sq by bus 71 toward Watertown Sq, or the 73 toward Waverley. Get off along Mt Auburn St, at Brattle St, and walk in the direction of travel to the main entrance. Drivers can park on most cemetery roads.

Accessibility
You can spot a variety of bird species from Mt Auburn's extensive network of wheelchair-accessible paved roads and paths (though note that the terrain can be hilly in places).

When to go
Mt Auburn is a noted stopover for northbound spring migrants, making mid-April to mid-May the busiest season for birders. However, many species can be seen year-round, including cardinals, blue jays, chickadees, goldfinches and red-tailed hawks.

Further information
• Free to visitors.
• Open year-round.
• No specialist facilities.
• Restaurant, supermarket and hotels nearby.
• www.mountauburn. org

Other Historic Massachusetts Sites

Halibut Point State Park, Rockport

Jutting into the Atlantic at the northern tip of Cape Ann, rugged Halibut Point was the site of a granite quarry until the industry collapsed in 1929. It's now a birding hot-spot, especially so between late autumn and early spring (roughly November to April) when large numbers of cormorants, loons, grebes, ducks, gannets and other seabirds feed in the productive waters just offshore.

Don't miss

Descending to the rocky shore for water-level birding.

Daniel Webster Wildlife Sanctuary, Marshfield

Midway between Boston and Cape Cod, this Mass Audubon Society preserve was once the property of English settler William Thomas, and later of the 19th-century lawyer-statesperson Daniel Webster. Its wetlands, grasslands and woodlands attract many year-round and seasonal species, including shorebirds, songbirds, raptors and wild turkeys. There are 3.6 miles (5.7km) of trails and two observation blinds.

Don't miss

Watching for northern harriers from Fox Hill observation deck.

Watch the cock-of-the-rock dance in the Andean highlands

 Endemic species, rare spectacles, cloud forest

 July to September

The fiery flash of an Andean cock-of-the-rock flitting through the cloud forests is one of the most iconic sights of the Ecuadorian highlands. So when you first catch a glimpse of this Latin American beauty, you might struggle to comprehend why it's known, in Ecuador's Indigenous Kichwa language, as a 'pig bird' (cuchi pishku). The seemingly discourteous name will make much more sense, however, if you're lucky enough to come across one of the near-mythical lek display sites, where male birds perform courtship dances amid choruses of distinctively porcine squeals.

Mindo's world-class birding
Just two hours' drive from Quito, Ecuador's capital, the town of Mindo is officially counted among the best birding sights in the world – it's frequently a clear world champion in the National Audubon Society's annual Christmas bird count.

More than 600 bird species have been listed in this area, but it is the cock-of-the-rock that captures the imagination. This is as much for the male's startling appearance – with its crimson upper-half, jet-black wings, smoky-grey back and puffy red crest, so large that it almost conceals the beak – as for the dancing courtship rituals that are performed at secret leks deep in the forest.

The Andean cock-of-the-rock is relatively common within its range (which stretches from Bolivia to Venezuela), and most birders who take an early morning hike along the cloud forest valleys around Mindo town are blessed with a sighting or two. However, if you're lucky enough to encounter

Right: A male Andean cock-of-the-rock performs for an audience

Below: Cloud forest, the bird's habitat, is extremely biodiverse

Q&A

When did you start birding?
My family moved to Mindo when I was a little girl and I grew up watching – and listening to – birds. It seemed then that that was all that Mindo had!

Do you think the people of Mindo are proud of the birding status of their town?
I think half the people of Mindo have a real love for birds...the other half are just enjoying the adventure!

Most sought after here?
The rarest and most special sightings are probably banded ground cuckoo, cloud-forest pygmy owl, dark-backed wood quail, scaled antpitta and ocellated tapaculo.

Apart from cock-of-the-rock, what's your favourite local bird?
I can pass hours watching the golden-headed quetzal – or guajalito (as it's locally known) – and listening to its song. This beautiful bird is never far from my mind.

Julia Patiño, MindoXtrem Birds guide

© David Havel / Shutterstock; GTW / Shutterstock; Holger Kirk / Shutterstock

Left: Rufous-tailed hummingbirds at a feeder in Mindo

Right: A spectacled bear cub in Ecuador's Maquipucuna Cloudforest Reserve

Don't Miss

➜ Spotting the pale, staring eyes of a nesting female cock-of-the-rock

➜ Catching sight of hummingbirds – about 40 species – flitting like sword-fencing fairies

➜ Adding 27 tanager species and six antpittas to your sightings list

one of the ceremonial courtship performances (usually seen at dawn or dusk between July and September), you've been privileged to witness one of the most mysterious avian rituals of the Andean highlands.

A colourful courtship

What might sound at first like a truckload of squealing piglets turns out, on closer inspection, to be a fluttering, bobbing, hopping congregation of a dozen or more crimson-orange males – each a little larger than a European thrush – single-mindedly trying

to catch the interest of females. There's a hint of desperation about the whole thing, but also a sense of joy to the ceremonial lekking – which, after all, comes from the Swedish word for 'play'.

During bouts of dancing that might last several hours, males will sometimes pair up in an effort to outdo their opponents. Researchers believe that rather than acting like duelling disco-dancers, they are forming a sort of coalition – one that allows the two performers to monopolise the best branches and maintain the all-important centre-stage position.

After mating, the females lay their two eggs in mud nests constructed under cliff overhangs or in caves. Hiking through the dramatic valleys around Mindo, you might come across these sites and get a birding thrill of a very different sort, in seeing the comparatively very dull-looking 'hen-of-the-rock' feeding her hatchlings.

Find Your Joy

Getting there
Quito's international airport is a convenient hub. From Quito, public buses or taxis run to

Mindo in about two hours; buses stop on the main road, where local taxis are waiting to take you into town. MindoXtrem Birds (www.mindoxtreme.com) here offers specialist birding tours.

Accessibility
The forest trails are virtually inaccessible to anyone with limited mobility, but in Mindo

town, accessible hotel and resort gardens offer bountiful sightings of spectacular birdlife.

When to go
The cock-of-the-rock courtship displays tend to take place between July and September but Mindo's rainy season (between October and May) is the best time for birding in general. National

Audubon Society bird-counts take place in December.

Further information
• Many trails are free; private reserves may charge a fee.
• Year-round.
• No specialist facilities.
• Mindo has accommodation, restaurants and bars.

© Angela N Perryman / Shutterstock. Animallraphy / Shutterstock

Other Ecuadorian Birding Sites

Maquipucuna Reserve, Pichincha Province

An hour north of Mindo, this secluded ecolodge on a 22-sq-mile (57-sq-km) reserve is an exclusive base for seeing the region's birds (including the cock-of-the-rock). It's also the best place on the planet to spot Andean spectacled bears; during the wild avocado season (roughly August and November), the resident population of around 50 is massively boosted by migratory bears.

Don't miss

Watching hummingbirds buzzing around feeders and flowers from the dining room.

Siempre Verde, Imbabura Province

North of Maquipucuna, Siempre Verde is a jungle-lover's dream hideaway, in pristine cloud forest at the head of spectacular Intag Valley (one of Ecuador's richest, and least known, birding areas). Siempre Verde means 'always green' and – despite the fact that you're almost on the equator – there's a feeling of perpetual springtime here: wake to birdsong, trek deserted trails and spend cosy evenings by a log fire.

Don't miss

Snagging a sighting of the rarely-spotted leymebamba antpitta.

Track toucans in the mountain forests of Monteverde

 Engaging the senses, forest bathing, wild nature

 December to April

COSTA RICA

It's early morning in the cloud forests of Curi-Cancha Reserve, in Costa Rica's Monteverde region. The root-laced trails are flanked by super-sized tropical vegetation, dripping with moisture and shrouded in ethereal swirling mist. Amid the invigorating soundtrack of wake-up whistles, whoops, chirrups, caws and trills, one distinctive call stands out – that of the equally singular keel-billed toucan, balanced on a high branch like a flamboyant flower.

Even among the profusion of Costa Rican birdlife, this showstopping toucan commands attention. With its outsized rainbow-coloured bill, blue legs and yellow face, and throat adorning jet-black plumage, it is the epitome of a tropical bird, at once familiar yet also thrillingly exotic. Smart and sociable, it communicates with its companions with squawks, croaks and clucks, head quizzically tilted to one side. Watching it hop through the lush foliage in search of the juiciest fruits, resorting to aerial acrobatics to reach them, it's impossible not to smile.

The keel-billed is just one member of a large avian family. There are more than 40 species of toucan, and Costa Rica is home to six of them, including the chestnut-mandibled and evocatively named fiery-billed aracari toucans, plus two species of toucanets.

A ranch in the clouds

Monteverde sits high on the country's mountainous spine, where moist air from the Caribbean collides with dry air from the Pacific, creating a cloud-covered biodiversity hot-spot. Here, Curi-Cancha is a cattle ranch turned private

Right: Keel-billed toucans use that lightweight bill to break up fruit before eating

Below: Toucan couples nest in disused woodpecker holes in trees

Q&A

The best thing about toucans?
Their beautiful call every morning!

Tell me a fun toucan fact!
A toucan's large, colourful bill can be almost half its length

Why so big and bright?
Toucans are omnivores and their bills are designed to deal with fruit, rodents, smaller birds, frogs, lizards – even bats. Made of keratin, the bills are not as heavy as they look, and their vibrant colours an advertisement for a mate and a warning to rivals. And toucans use them to adjust their body temperature, much like an elephant uses its ears.

Any tips for photographing them?
Toucans are at their most active in early mornings and late afternoons. They can be skittish, so be patient and use a long lens because they tend to perch high in the canopy.

Roy Porras, Monteverde specialist guide

© Ondrej Prosicky / Shutterstock; Wondry / Shutterstock; Josh Miller Photography / Getty Images/Aurora Open

reserve that limits visitor numbers to minimise the effect on wildlife and on the trails that wind through primary, secondary and open forest.

Exploring this primordial world is a multisensory experience, a chance to connect to untamed nature. Pause to marvel at towering trees trapped in the ruthless embrace of strangler figs, at lofty branches festooned with bromeliads, luxuriant feather-like ferns and dainty miniature orchids. In higher elevations, keep an eye out for the elusive northern emerald toucanet – less bold than its larger cousins, but no less beautiful in its subtle leaf-green plumage.

Right: A northern emerald toucanet

Far right: A scarlet macaw in Costa Rica's Corcovado National Park

A nocturnal symphony

After dark, the forest takes on an entirely different aspect. Enveloped in inky blackness, close your eyes, breathe in the heady aroma of damp earth, and open yourself to the magnified nocturnal noises – the frog chorus, the chirp of crickets, the rustle of vegetation.

A shaft of moonlight or the torch of your eagle-eyed guide might pick out a somnolent three-toed sloth on its twig bed, or the enormous golden eyes of a startled kinkajou, a captivating cross between a monkey and a small bear. Or you might catch a keel-billed toucan in repose – as flexible as a yogi, with its head turned at a sharp angle so that its long bill rests along its back, its tail folded backwards, inquiring eyes closed until sunlight dapples the forest again.

Don't Miss

→ **Looking out for tiny jewel-coloured hummingbirds**

→ **Whizzing over the forest canopy on a zip line**

→ **Sampling the local organic coffee, chocolate and cheese**

Find Your Joy

Getting there
Monteverde is 91 miles (147km) northwest of the capital, San José. The Curi-Cancha Reserve is around 2 miles (3km) from the small town of Santa Elena; to reach Santa Elena from San José, take a bus (5–6 hours), a shared shuttle (4–5 hours), or arrange a private transfer (3–4 hours). Curi-Cancha offers group and private guided birding tours (advance booking essential), but you can also go in with independent guides, and visitors can walk the trails solo during the day.

Accessibility
The reserve offers guided tours in electric golf buggies for people with limited mobility.

When to go
The best time to visit Monteverde is from December to April, during Costa Rica's dry season – March and April are usually the driest months. The toucan nesting season is April to June.

Further information
• Admission charge.
• Year-round.
• No specialist facilities.
• Santa Elena has restaurants and rooms.
• www. reservacuricancha.com

© Milan Zygmunt / Shutterstock; Mateo Simoni / Getty Images

Other Costa Rican Birding Hot-spots

Arenal Volcano National Park, Alajuela

Arenal Volcano's postcard-perfect cone – resting, for now – looms over the town of La Fortuna in northwest Costa Rica. Five of the country's six toucan species call its namesake national park home, including the emblematic keel-billed toucan. Get active hiking, horse riding, mountain biking, rappelling and ziplining, or kayaking and windsurfing on Lake Arenal. The region's natural hot springs are perfect for easing weary muscles afterwards.

Don't miss
Spotting rare yellow-eared toucanets.

Corcovado National Park, Osa Peninsula

In Costa Rica's remote southwestern corner, Corcovado is a mix of steamy rainforest, languid rivers and dense mangroves, all ringed by Robinson Crusoe-esque beaches – a place where you're more likely to hear the screech of scarlet macaws than fellow travellers. One of the most biodiverse places on the planet, its multiple habitats shelter a staggering variety of flora and fauna, including 370 bird species.

Don't miss
Glimpses of brightly coloured trogons, including the endemic Baird's.

Spectate squadrons of pelicans and seabirds in Baja California Sur

 Aerobatic displays, warm water, marine life

 September to May

MEXICO

It's dawn in Loreto, looking out over the Sea of Cortez. Gliding into view, their heads tucked back between their shoulders, is a squadron of pelicans, scouting the shoreline in search of shoals of fish. Then, one by one, they fold their wings into a W shape and drop through the sky and into the sea at 40mph (65km/h). Soon, pelicans are plummeting into the frothing water at all angles and seagulls are circling in search of an easy meal.

The world's aquarium

This drama plays out every day along the shore of the Sea of Cortez, a strip of sea between mainland Mexico and the Baja California peninsula that averages just 100 miles (160km) in width. Compact it may be, but this is one of the most biodiverse marine habitats on the planet, nicknamed the 'world's aquarium'

by oceanographer Jacques Cousteau. More than half a dozen species of whale feed or breed here, including giant blue whales. Sea lions haul out on the desert islands along the coast. Under the waves, great schools of mobula rays and voracious Humboldt squid thrive. Of the 900 species of fish that call the Sea of Cortez home, 77 are unique to the place.

It is this rich life that supports such sea birds as the brown and white pelicans plus cormorants, frigate birds and the yellow-footed gulls that are only found in the gulf. The pelicans are more prehistoric than pretty, inspiring awe and a little caution, courtesy of their 8ft (2.5m) wingspans, self-confident attitude, and formidable bills. The design dates back 30 million years: pelicans are descended from dinosaurs rather than soaring reptilian pterosaurs (the two groups separated from

Right: Brown pelicans diving for fish off Baja California Sur

Below: A Gulf of California feeding frenzy; the throat pouches are used for catching but not storing fish

© Mike Laptev / Shutterstock; Mario Vargas9 / / Shutterstock; Micah Riegner

Q&A

What can people expect in Baja California Sur?
Warm days, whales and fun, relatively easy birding.

What birds can be seen?
In the Sierra de La Laguna Biosphere Reserve at the southern tip of the peninsula you can see endemic birds, such as the striking Xantus's hummingbird, Cape pygmy-owl, gray thrasher, the San Lucas robin, and Baird's junco. Around La Paz there are some mudflats to see a good diversity of shorebirds and in the mangroves you can see Ridgway's rails and mangrove warblers. Plus the two species of pelican: the brown pelican, which is a resident along the coast, and the migratory American white.

It's not just about birds in Baja, is it?
No! I recommend going to Magdalena Bay to see the grey whales. One approached our boat; it was like a big puppy wanting its belly rubbed!

Micah Riegner, guide with www.fieldguides.com

Left: Grey whales give birth and nurse in three locations off Baja California Sur

Right: Pink flamingos in the Yucatán's Celestún Biosphere Reserve

Don't Miss

→ **Whale watching from January to April, when you might spot blue, fin, humpback or sperm whales**

→ **Joining a boat or kayak tour of the islands, camping overnight on the beaches**

→ **Enjoying crowd-free birding at Sierra de La Laguna Biosphere Reserve**

a common ancestor some 250 million years ago) and they wouldn't look out of place in a *Jurassic Park* movie.

Exploring Baja California Sur

Parque Nacional Bahía de Loreto protects more than 800 sq miles (2000 sq km) of this marine ecosystem, including several islands that the pelicans share with cormorants, blue-footed boobies and sea lion colonies. The park is now a Unesco World Heritage Site; and Loreto, just outside, is its tourism hub. To the south, state capital La Paz is another base for

marine adventures. Sea-kayaking trips out to such islands as Isla Espíritu Santo (off La Paz) and Isla Carmen (off Loreto) are popular ways of watching birdlife and encountering marine mammals. Watch out for the male bull sea lions, which are disconcertingly large and protective. If you're very lucky, you may see whales breach, their giant flukes slapping down onto the sea's surface.

Kayakers can camp on the beaches of these islands. Haul up your kayak on the sand and pitch a tent, safe in the knowledge that there is minimal tidal range in this sea, meaning that you can wake up to sparkling blue water and the dawn diving display of the daredevil pelicans.

Continue south to the town of Santiago for the Sierra de La Laguna Biosphere Reserve, the prime birding location here. It's considered a 'sky island' because of the higher elevation habitat surrounded by desert.

Find Your Joy

Getting there
There are direct flights to the resort of Cabo San Lucas from several US cities but it's then a 7-hour

drive north to Loreto. La Paz receives flights from around a dozen Mexican cities, so changing from an international flight in Mexico City is an option. You'll need a rental car or to take buses; some tour operators, such as Wild Loreto, organise private (and pricey) shuttles from Cabo San Lucas and La Paz to Loreto.

Accessibility
Outside of the resorts, Baja California Sur is not well set up for people with a disability. There's very little infrastructure for birdwatching. Going with a guide is advised.

When to go
The months between December and April (winter in the northern hemisphere) offer the

most comfortable climate and the possibility of seeing whales in addition to birds.

Further information
• Operators such as Field Guides (www. fieldguides.com) host expert tours from La Paz and Santiago.
• www.visitbajasur.travel

© Jan-Dirk Hansen / Shutterstock; Jose de Jesus Churion Del / Shutterstock

Other Mexican Birding Sites

Celestún Biosphere Reserve, Yucatán

On the eastern side of the country, perched at the top of the Yucatán peninsula beside the Gulf of Mexico, Celestún is one of the most biodiverse places on the planet. Habitats stretch from dry forests, home to woodpeckers, orioles, flycatchers and pygmy owls, to rare mangroves filled with wetland birds. In total, there are more than 1100 species of bird in and around Celestún.

Don't miss
Never mind the pink flamingos, admire the unique Yucatan wren.

Cerro San Felipe, Oaxaca

Mountainous Oaxaca, in the south of Mexico, is renowned as a great birding destination, home to around 800 species of bird, with a large number of those being endemic to the region. The pine forests of Cerro San Felipe (also known as La Cumbre) are easily accessible from state capital Oaxaca City and offer red warblers, mountain trogons, sparrows, vireos and various hummingbirds.

Don't miss
Top of most lists of visitors to Oaxaca are blue-hued dwarf jays, endemic only to these highlands.

Marvel at a rainbow of macaws at the Chuncho clay lick

 Kaleidoscopic colours, Amazonian adventure, iconic wildlife

 November to June

PERU

Just getting to Peru's Tambopata region is an Amazon adventure in itself. You'll undoubtedly have had many incredible sightings by the time you arrive here by river, but nothing can prepare you for the sensory overload of visiting the clay licks in Reserva Nacional Tambopata, where a riot of vibrant colours, feathered mayhem and squawking pandemonium awaits.

A feathered frenzy
Towering 33ft (10m) high, Chuncho's eroded face plays host to one of the most spectacular wildlife shows on the planet. Arriving at the *collpa* (as the clay licks are known locally) around dawn, you'll stay quiet and secluded, close to the mineral-rich cliff-face as flocks of parakeets and parrots arrive. But these are just the opening act

for the real stars of this colourful avian carnival – it's never long before the macaws flock down in multicoloured squadrons.

The clay licks of the Tambopata region are visited by six species of macaw (scarlet, red-and-green, blue-and-yellow, red-bellied, blue-headed and chestnut-fronted) and eleven species of parrots, parakeets and parrotlets – including orange-cheeked, blue-headed and white-bellied parrots, dusky-headed, white-eyed and cobalt-winged parakeets and dusky-billed and Manu parrotlets.

A wealth of wildlife
Thanks in large part to ongoing work at Tambopata Research Center (owned by Peruvian ecotourism company Rainforest Expeditions), Reserva Nacional Tambopata has become celebrated as one of the world's richest areas of biodiversity. As

Right: The scarlet macaw is highly intelligent and sometimes described as 'sassy'

Below: Three species of macaw use the clay lick to counteract toxins from their diets

© Jan Korba / Shutterstock; czekma13 / Getty Images; Mark Green / Shutterstock

Q&A

It's the macaws that lure visitors to Tambopata. Are they your favourite?
I like all birds, but the lemon-throated barbet is a real beauty and the manakins (nine species here!) are such amazing dancers.

Most sought-after sightings?
Serious birders want to see antbirds, white-cheeked tody-flycatchers, band-tailed and round-tailed manakins… Of course, everybody loves the toucans and toucanets!

Tambopata Province is home to many Indigenous groups too, right?
The cultural life is most visible during the tough dry season (July and August), when communities go fishing or hunting, using just bows and arrows. Also, entire families collect the freshwater turtle eggs that are a valuable part of their diet.

Tambopata sounds like a real adventure…
It is! Visitors here are frequently astounded by iconic sightings of jaguars, ocelot and tapirs.

Erick Arguedas, Tambopata Research Center resident guide

Right: A giant otter in Tambopata's Sandoval Lake

Far right: A blue-headed macaw in Peru, a member of the mini-macaw family

many as 600 bird species have been recorded here, but if you can tear your eyes away from the birdlife for long enough, you're almost certain to see caiman, piranha, giant otters, capybara (the world's largest rodent) and some of the region's eight monkey species, including the astounding howler (once heard, never forgotten). And almost half of all guests at Tambopata Research Center Lodge are privileged to see wild jaguars along the riverbanks.

Many experts claim that birds visit Tambopata's clay licks because they offer access to nutrients that may counteract the toxins in a diet of seeds and berries, but researchers at Texas A&M University believe they have established that birds gather here primarily because of the high sodium content in the soil.

The mystery is still under debate but, whatever the reason, macaws have been recorded flying up to 62 miles (100km) to get to what appear to be

extremely boisterous 'parties' at the Tambopata *collpas*. They squabble and jostle for prime position on the near vertical cliff-face, creating a shimmering palette across the cliffs as they cluster in rainbow-hued mobs.

Plan to stick around and enjoy as much of the show as possible: occasionally the finale is a dramatic explosion of colours, as the birds glimpse the shadow of a swooping harpy eagle and take to the skies. Occasionally, the eagle is quick enough to make a kill among the squawking turmoil of scattering birds.

Don't Miss

➡ **Spotting wild jaguars – Tambopata offers a high chance of sightings**

➡ **Hearing the howls of Amazonian giant otters, aka *lobos del rio* (river wolves)**

➡ **Sighting the spectacularly prehistoric-looking hoatzin**

Find Your Joy

Getting there
The city of Puerto Maldonado is the gateway to Tambopata (by which the river, the province

and the national reserve are all known). Flights from Lima to Puerto Maldonado take 1½ hours; it's then an hour by road and 2½ hours by boat to the Tambopata Research Center Lodge (www. rainforestexpeditions. com), which arranges visits to the clay licks .

Accessibility
Remote Tambopata

is accessible only by a road-and-river journey. Rainforest Cruises (www. rainforestcruises.com) run trips on the Peruvian Amazon that are suitable for people with mobility issues, and can provide expert birding guides.

When to go
Sightings are good all year but the rainy season (November to June), when

trees are fruiting, offers added excitement in the nesting birds, baby monkeys and increased visibility of reptiles and amphibians.

Further information
• Year-round.
• Hides available.
• Tambopata Research Center Lodge has accommodation, a restaurant and a bar.

© Christian Vinces / Shutterstock; Heather Paul / Getty Images

Other Tambopata Clay Licks

Collpa Colorado

Three times as high as Chuncho, Colorado is the world's largest *collpa* (though it's in permanent transformation and some parts have lately been recolonised by vegetation). It's deep in virgin rainforest and close to the Bolivian border, so it takes determination to get here, but the reward is sighting chestnut-fronted, red-bellied and blue-headed macaws nibbling at the clay.

Don't miss

Spotting the extremely rare blue-headed macaw, a frequent Colorado visitor.

Collpa Ocho Gallinas

This popular *collpa* is one of Latin America's most active macaw observation points. It's an hour by boat from riverside Filadelfia (itself about an hour's drive southwest of Puerto Maldonado). While it's smaller than Colorado and Chuncho, Ocho Gallinas is a photographers' favourite, with easy viewing from the shore of a river-island facing the clay lick.

Don't miss

Staying till late morning to see herds of white-lipped peccaries devouring the nutrient-rich clay.

Witness a mass congregation of sandhill cranes

 Migratory visitors, engaging your senses, stunning landscapes

 February to April

USA

It's a scene to make birders go weak at the knees: thousands of sandhill cranes fill an empty cornfield near the Platte River in central Nebraska. Grouped in clusters, the lanky grey birds bend their slender necks toward the rows of short, pale-yellow stalks. They peck here and there, scarfing down kernels of corn left by farmers the previous autumn.

As the sun dips closer to the horizon, the birds' internal clocks respond to the impending darkness. On instinct, a few individuals take to the sky and venture south toward the safety of the braided river's sandy islands. Another group soon does the same, followed by another and another, until the sky is full of flapping wings.

A roost on the river
Considering their large size – between 3ft and 4ft tall (around 1m) – sandhill cranes are remarkably elegant, and the geometric pattern of crimson and white patches around their eyes only adds to their distinguished aesthetic. With wingspans of some 7ft (2m) and their skinny legs stretched long behind them, the flocking birds create a dazzling spectacle. But it's the sound that really thrills: together, the flying cranes create a cacophonous chorus with their sustained, rattling calls. Once they reach the water, they descend and congregate en masse in open, shallow areas of the

Right: Adult sandhill cranes have a red flash on their heads

Below: Migrating sandhill cranes flying over Nebraskan cornfields

Q&A

Have sandhill cranes put Central Nebraska on the map?
The spring migration in the central Platte River Valley is the largest gathering of cranes in the world. It is one of the greatest migration spectacles our planet has to offer.

What's the vibe?
Visitors can find subtle connections to the cranes, whether it's the joy of their dance, their playfulness as they toss corncobs into the air with their beaks or the annoyance of bonded pairs trying to claim a space among an ever-growing crowd of birds. I love the reflection of humanity you can see in their interactions.

What's special about Platte River?
These sandy channels are so dynamic; shifting and reshaping with the ebb and flow of Rocky Mountain meltwater. The cranes are special, but the river holds a charm all its own.

Cody Wagner, Iain Nicolson Audubon Center at Rowe Sanctuary conservation programme manager

© kojihirano / Shutterstock; Imageinit / Shutterstock; ShayneKayePhoto / Shutterstock; marekuliasz / Shutterstock

Left: Sunset over the Platte River

Right: Hundreds of thousands of sandhill cranes migrate annually

pit stop in Nebraska to rest and refuel in this bottleneck section of the Central Flyway.

The first sandhills appear between the towns of North Platte and Grand Island in February, and continue arriving in droves throughout March and into April, gaining an estimated 20% of their body weight during the three to four weeks they spend here – this extra heft sustains them for the rest of their migration. At the peak in mid-March, some 500,000 sandhills may gather along the Platte River; over the course of the spring, roughly a million will pass through the area.

The oldest known sandhill crane fossil is more than 2.5 million years old, but some evidence suggests these birds are much older than that. Their annual arrival not only inspires awe and wonder, but also serves as a tangible connection to the past – to a migration that was old before the first humans walked in the Americas.

Don't Miss

→ **Listening to the cranes' trilling bugle calls**

→ **Watching the sun rise or set over the Platte River**

→ **Enjoying the solitude of a viewing-blind in the morning quiet**

Platte to roost for the night. Here, they have safety in numbers and can easily see and hear any approaching predators. This unique protective habitat is one of the key reasons why they return year after year.

Lords of the Central Flyway

Sandhill cranes spend the winter in the warm climates of Mexico, Florida, Texas and Central California. But in early spring, they begin the long migration to breeding grounds in Alaska, Canada and parts of the northern US. Along the way, many make a

Find Your Joy

Getting there
Fly into Omaha's Eppley Airfield, then rent a car and head west on I-80. Pull off anywhere between Grand Island and North Platte to see cranes, or head to Wood River's Crane Trust Nature & Visitor Center (www.cranetrust.org), and Gibbon's Iain Nicolson Audubon Center at Rowe Sanctuary (https://rowe.audubon.org).

Accessibility
Sandhill cranes are so abundant hereabouts you don't even have to get out of the car to see them. Popular viewing platforms (like Gibbon's Richard Plautz Crane Viewing Site) have ramps, flat trails and paved parking lots.

When to go
Sandhill cranes – and, occasionally, endangered whooping cranes – touch down here from late February to early April; numbers peak mid-March.

Further information
• River access is free.
• Viewing blinds, tours, classes and visitor centres at the Crane Trust and Iain Nicolson Audubon Center.
• Hotels and restaurants nearby in Grand Island, Kearney and Hastings.
• www.outdoornebraska.gov

Other US Migration Locations

Whitewater Draw Wildlife Area, Arizona

Many sandhill cranes spend the winter basking in the balmy weather of southern Arizona – and the 600-acre (243-hectare) Whitewater Draw Wildlife Area in McNeal is one of the best places to spot them. The birds spend their days snacking on crops in the surrounding agricultural fields, then return to roost in Whitewater's shallow pools and marshland each night. They begin arriving in October and stay through February.

Don't miss
The Wings Over Willcox Birding and Nature Festival in January.

Lamar, Colorado

See tens of thousands of bright-white snow geese gather in southeastern Colorado, near the towns of Lamar, Kit Carson and Cheyenne Wells, in January and February during their annual migration. Here, the birds live up to their name by turning entire fields and lakes white, making it look as though they're blanketed with snow.

Don't miss
Lamar's High Plains Snow Goose Festival, held in early February to celebrate the birds' arrival.

Experience spring migration at an Ontario birding hot-spot

 Migratory visitors, rare encounters, engaging your senses

 Late April to late May

CANADA

Each spring, billions of birds embark on the long and arduous journey from South America to their preferred breeding grounds in North America, and there are few places better than Point Pelee to bear witness to one of nature's greatest migrations. In fact, the national park's unique geography makes this one of the region's very best birding locations.

Located between two major migratory flyways, Point Pelee comprises a long spit of land jutting into Lake Erie's northwest shore, making it the first piece of land that exhausted migrants see after the long overnight flight over Erie's waters. Pelee's lakeside location also keeps the temperature relatively cool, stunting the growth of spring foliage and allowing the birds to be seen with fewer obstructions.

Morning flight

Before sunrise, in a flutter of anticipation, birders load into the electric shuttle that departs from the visitor centre, then wind silently down the road while the songs of thrushes ring through the forest, disembarking just a short distance from the tip of the spit. The rising sun paints the waves of Lake Erie in brilliant hues of orange and red, and the chatter of birders is met by the soft, melodic symphony of hundreds of songbirds flying overhead.

With binoculars in hand, avian enthusiasts stand at the tip of Point Pelee and begin calling out rare and exciting birds as they fly in off the lake. Stunning Blackburnian warblers flash their flame-orange throats as they swoop in; ruby-throated hummingbirds shine like jewels in the morning sun. Lucky

Right: A beautiful Blackburnian warbler in Point Pelee National Park

Below: Boardwalks enable visitors to get deep into the wetlands of Point Pelee

Q&A

Why do you love birding at Point Pelee?
The diversity and abundance of migrating birds, and Point Pelee's southern flair. Where else in Ontario can you go birding among cacti?

How can visitors minimise their impact?
Migration is a costly journey that claims the lives of millions of birds annually; a safe, natural stopover like Point Pelee is crucial for their survival. During the spring or fall, it's important to not approach or harass the exhausted birds: stay on the marked trails, and don't walk on the sand-spit at the tip until later in the day.

Any tips for visitors?
The birds are active before sunrise (as are the other birders!), so waking up early will guarantee a better birding day – and increase your chances of getting parking as far south down the point as possible!

Henrique Pacheco, Ontario naturalist and bird expert

© Chiyacat / Shutterstock; Willem Span; Bob Hilscher / Shutterstock

birders might even catch a glimpse of a cerulean warbler as it sings its buzzy song from the canopy. There's a tangible sense of community, as birders of all experience levels share stories and sightings while intently scanning the incoming waves of birds. Morning is the perfect time to experience the magic of the spring migration, and friendly regulars are always willing to lend a helping hand to aspiring birders.

Explore on foot

Point Pelee offers several walking trails where you can immerse yourself in the joys of the spring migration, and perhaps share your latest sightings with fellow birders. From exploring the oldest forests in the park along the Woodland Nature Trail to walking the boardwalk Marsh Trail through wetland habitats, Point Pelee offers a wide variety of ecosystems, appealing to

Right: A male cerulean warbler in Point Pelee; the birds overwinter in the Andes

Far right: Prothonotary warblers get their name from robes worn by papal clerks

hundreds of different bird species.

Dotted with interpretive signage, the DeLaurier Homestead Trail is a favourite among birders and offers fantastic opportunities to see rare species like the prothonotary warbler, whose golden plumage shines bright even in the dark swamps it calls home. There are few greater pleasures than walking DeLaurier as dozens of songbirds whistle sweet songs and flutter their delicate wings in the canopy above.

Don't Miss

➡ **Listening to the chorus of rails, bitterns and herons in the marsh at dusk**

➡ **Scanning the skies for migrating raptors along the lakeshore**

➡ **Catching the Point Pelee Festival of Birds in early May**

Find Your Joy

Getting there
Point Pelee is a four-hour drive southwest of Toronto via Hwy 401, and a one-hour drive from Windsor. A bus runs from Windsor to the nearby town of Leamington, from where you can take a taxi into the park.

Accessibility
Many of the park's trails can accommodate wheelchairs, and free all-terrain wheelchairs are available from the visitor centre. The shuttle from here to Point Pelee's tip is also accessible, as are bathrooms throughout the park.

When to go
While spring migration in Point Pelee lasts from April to late May, early to mid-May sees incredible species diversity and peak volume of birds in the park.

Further information
• Admission charge; annual passes available.
• No specialist facilities.
• Book early for the park's A-frame tents; Leamington has plentiful hotels.
• Restaurants just outside the park entrance and in Leamington.
• parks.canada.ca

Other Ontario Birding Locations

Rondeau Provincial Park

Just an hour northeast of Point Pelee, on a sand-spit extending into Lake Erie, Rondeau is also a must-visit during the spring migration, and offers great birding at other times of the year too. The park protects some of Ontario's last remaining old-growth Carolinian forest, a habitat which serves as an ideal summer nursery for many bird species – from red-headed woodpeckers to Acadian flycatchers.

Don't Miss

Listening for the song of prothonotary warblers on the Tulip Tree Trail.

Long Point Provincial Park

This Lake Erie sand-spit is another exceptional birding hot-spot. The various research stations here are well known for their work in monitoring and banding migratory species, like grasshopper sparrows and golden-winged warblers; see the birds up close during banding demonstrations and learn more about migration, bird science and conservation from friendly staff.

Don't Miss

Scouring the wetlands for marsh birds like the American bittern.

Watch the ostrich-like rhea stride across Patagonian plains

CHILE

 Hiking, diverse wildlife, awe-inspiring landscapes

 October to March

As you travel along the road to Torres del Paine National Park, the landscape becomes increasingly wild and rugged; and even before you reach the park entrance, wildlife appears. A Darwin's (or lesser) rhea – one of the continent's largest birds, just behind its own close relative, the greater rhea – lopes along the undulating plain, its head bobbing and its wings spread, greyish-brown feathers bouncing with every step.

It's thrilling to see this massive bird running – or even just strolling – across the landscape, sometimes solitary, sometimes in pairs or small groups. But rheas aren't Torres del Paine's only avian attraction. Overhead, an Andean condor soars, its massive wingspan outlined against jagged mountain peaks. On the steppe below, more condors tear at the remnants of some prey, dwarfing the crested caracaras (by no means small birds) also hoping for a taste.

A glorious living wilderness

Torres del Paine translates to 'towers of blue' in a blend of Spanish and the Indigenous Tehuelche language. The name refers to the three sheer granite pinnacles that rise up to 9462ft (2884m) from the Paine Massif alongside the equally spectacular Cuernos del Paine ('horns of Paine').

Beneath this dramatic backdrop are sapphire glacial lakes, wild cascading rivers, patches of woodland and vast plains covered with a mix of grasses and shrubland. Pumas roam here, though they are difficult to spot, as are the shy native huemul deer. Andean foxes are bolder, emerging from the brush to hunt

Right: Male rheas incubate many eggs from several females in a single nest

Below: A resilient rhea in Torres del Paine National Park

Q&A

What's special about birding here?
It's probably is the best place in the world to see condors. Torres del Paine also has one of the largest densities of rhea in Chile. They can reach almost 40mph (64km/h), so you have to have your camera ready.

What's the best time to visit?
The southern hemisphere spring is good because it's a time of breeding, but I also recommend visiting in winter for wildlife close encounters. You won't see as many species, but there's a welcome quiet, and the park is so spectacular – covered with snow.

Do you have a favourite bird?
My personal favourite is the torrent duck, which lives exclusively in whitewater rivers and can dive against very fast currents. It's an example of going against the flow for a good purpose.

Raffaele Di Biase, BirdsChile cofounder, director and guide

© Ondrej Prosicky / Shutterstock; Luciana Tancredo / Shutterstock; Foto 4440 / Shutterstock

Left: The granite peaks of Torres del Paine

Right: Alpacas in Lauca National Park

A conservation success story, with challenges

The Torres del Paine region was once the home of the nomadic Tehuelche people. Later, Chileans of European origin established sheep ranches in the area and began fencing off their territories. The national park was established in 1959 to preserve the magnificent landscapes and allow for the free movement of wildlife through a large variety of habitats.

But as the park's popularity has grown, Torres del Paine's fragile ecosystems have come under threat from human-caused erosion and forest fires. One accommodation that has made an effort to minimise its effect is EcoCamp Patagonia, where guests stay in geodesic domes built on wooden platforms. Nestled among shrubby trees on a hillside at the heart of the park, it's an ideal base for birdwatching, with many species commonly seen just steps from the domes.

Don't Miss

→ **Watching condors soaring up among the peaks**

→ **Seeing flamingos take flight from an alpine lake**

→ **Hiking alongside pure blue icebergs at Lago Grey**

and scavenge, scamper across the landscape or loll by the roadside. Llama-like guanacos abound – grazing, sparring, mating, resting, always alert to predators.

And everywhere there are birds – over 100 species. Upland geese wade in the shallows of lakes, the females reddish-brown, the males mostly white. Austral parakeets – the world's southernmost parrots – perch in woodlands, bright green with red breasts and tailfeathers. In the salt lakes in the east, Chilean flamingos feed, occasionally spreading their wings in dramatic flight.

Find Your Joy

Getting there
The park is 186 miles (300km) from the nearest airport in Punta Arenas, and 47 miles (76km) from Puerto Natales, from where buses into the park take two to 4½ hours (destination depending). Park admission varies, depending on length of stay and nationality (Chilean or foreign); advance ticket purchase is required (via www.aspticket.cl).

Accessibility
Torres del Paine's terrain is wild and rugged, but you can see spectacular views and wildlife when driving the park's roads; several overlooks and lake and lagoon shores are also accessible to those with limited mobility.

When to go
High season (December to early March) brings warm weather, green landscapes and abundant wildlife. Mid-October to December sees an explosion of new life.

Further information
• Admission charge.
• Open year-round.
• No specialist facilities.
• The park has hotels, campsites and *refugios* (hikers' hostels), most offering food.
• www.parquetorresdel paine.cl

© Philip Lee Harvey / Lonely Planet; Dmitry Chulov / Shutterstock

Other Chilean Birding Hot-spots

Chiloé Island, Los Lagos

Just south of Chile's Lake District, Chiloé is a place of beauty and magic. Lush, green and often shrouded by mist, it's home to many birds, from forest and wetland species to shorebirds scurrying across sandy beaches and ibises perched on urban rooftops.

Don't miss

A boat tour of the islands in seabird-rich Puñihuil Bay, the only place in the world where Humboldt and Magellanic penguins nest side by side.

Lauca National Park, Arica y Parinacota

This stunning park in Chile's far north preserves a high-altitude landscape of snowcapped volcanoes, Altiplano (Andean plateau), lava fields and lakes. It's home to more than 140 bird species, as well as other wildlife, including guanaco, vicuña and viscacha (a rare rodent with rabbit-like ears).

Don't miss

The chance to spot all three of Chile's flamingo species – Chilean, James's and Andean – which often feed at lakes such as Lauca's Chungará.

Find albatrosses & penguins on an isolated archipelago

 Rugged landscapes, close encounters, splendid isolation

 October to March

FALKLAND ISLANDS

Hiking over wind-blasted hills between clumps of canary-yellow gorse and bristly tussock grass, you'll hear a rookery long before you see it. First a cackling babble, punctuated by the demanding chirp of hungry chicks, and then perhaps an outraged squawk as a dispute erupts between a haughty albatross and its belligerent rockhopper penguin neighbour.

After spending three quarters of their year wandering over the open seas without touching land, more than 70% of the world's black-browed albatrosses return to nesting sites in the Falklands every September. They are arguably the most elegant of all seabirds – their white breasts as crisp as five-star-hotel sheets, their beaks a demure peach blush, and their flick of smudged eyeliner as alluring

as a fashion model's. Alongside them, with demonic red eyes and dishevelled yellow crests, rockhopper penguins make an almost comical counterpoint.

A lonely paradise for an albatross

Lost in the South Atlantic, about 300 miles (480km) east of Argentine Patagonia and about 750 miles (1200km) from the Antarctic Peninsula's northern tip, the Falklands – a British Overseas Territory of over 740 islands – are so far off the beaten track that few visitors make it here. But this remote location is also the ace up their sleeve. The nutrient-rich waters here are a paradise for fish and the predators that feed on them, and the Falklands are almost sinking under the weight of their avian diversity: as well as the million-plus black-browed albatrosses, the 220 or

Right: A black-browed albatross on the Falkland Islands; chicks fledge in April and May

Below: Black-browed albatrosses usually mate for life and can live for up to 70 years

© Charles Bergman / Shutterstock; Danita Delimont / Shutterstock; Farjana.rahman / Shutterstock

Q&A

Why do you love the Falklands?
There are two main reasons. The first is the lack of people: often I can be completely alone with the birds. Second, and probably because of the first, is that I can get so close to them and sometimes they even approach me.

Best feathered Falklands friend?
It's hard to choose, but probably the striated caracara (also known as the Johnny rook). It's one of the rarest birds of prey and one of the most intelligent and inquisitive species. For photography, my favourite is the stunning imperial cormorant, with its vivid blue eyes and orange nasal knob.

Guess I should bring my camera...
Don't forget your wide-angle lens, too – the birds get so close that sometimes a zoom lens is too much!

Andy Pollard, Falklands Nature bird guide

so bird species include petrels, cormorants, plovers and five species of penguin.

But while there are birds in their millions, what you won't find here are crowds: the islands have a population of about 3500 and receive fewer than 65,000 annual visitors, mostly cruise passengers making only a brief stop. Even more thrillingly, this freedom from interference means the birds have never learned to fear humans. Although visitors are advised to keep at least 16ft (5m) away from wildlife, it seems the rules don't apply the other way round. Linger at the edge of a penguin colony and a resident will probably come to inspect you, making this a photography paradise to rival even the Galápagos Islands.

Bird species galore
When you've had your fill of albatrosses, there's masses more to see – from the breathtaking drama of over 200,000 sooty

Right: A group of gentoo penguins, fresh from the Falkland Islands' surf

Far right: Several seabirds call New Zealand's Otago Peninsula home

shearwaters returning to roost every evening on Kidney Island (said to be the spectacle that inspired Hitchcock's film *The Birds*), to strolling the sugary white sands of Bertha's Beach among 1000 gentoo penguins. Then there's the thrill of spotting black-necked swans and flightless steamer ducks around the lagoon at Whale Point. The Falklands might be challenging to get to, but once you've soaked up their rugged, unspoiled beauty and approachable wildlife you'll wonder why you didn't make it here sooner.

Don't Miss

→ **Visiting Steeple Jason Island, the world's largest black-browed albatross colony**

→ **Seeing the 'Big Five' Falklands penguins – king, gentoo, Magellanic, rockhopper and macaroni**

→ **Enjoying a pint at the pub in Stanley**

Find Your Joy

Getting there
Flights operate weekly from Santiago, Chile to Port Stanley Airport, from where shuttle buses run to the capital. UK Ministry of Defence flights also run from Brize Norton, Oxfordshire; book via the Falklands Government Office (www.falklands.gov.fk). Falklands travel is mainly by 4WD or boat; book birding tours with Falklands Nature (www.falklandsnature.com).

Accessibility
Rookery trips involve boat/off-road transport and hiking cross-country, but with advance notice, guides can gain clearance to drive vehicles closer than usual to the relatively flat paths that lead to some of the rookeries.

When to go
Breeding season is October to March, with the warmest temperatures and longest days in December and January. Eggs are laid in October and November; chicks hatch from December.

Further information
• Fee for sites on private land.
• Year-round.
• No specialist facilities.
• Accommodation and restaurants in Stanley.
• www.falklands conservation.com/birds

© Helifundk / Shutterstock; Menon van Coetham / Shutterstock

Other Places to See Albatrosses

South Georgia Island

This uninhabited British Overseas Territory, 850 miles (1370km) east of the Falklands in the South Atlantic, has been dubbed the 'Galápagos of the South' for the astonishing scale of its biodiversity. Home to around seven million penguins and a breeding ground for black-browed, grey-headed and wandering albatrosses, this is a see-before-you-die destination for any intrepid bird lover.

Don't miss

Being inspected by half a million king penguins at the St Andrews Bay colony.

Taiaroa Head, New Zealand

At the tip of the South Island's Otago Peninsula, Taiaroa is home to the world's only mainland royal albatross breeding colony. Here you can find the majestic northern royal albatross, one of the largest species, with a 10ft (3m) wingspan and delicate pink beak. View them from the Royal Albatross Centre, which has an accessible observatory and a livestreaming nest camera.

Don't miss

Taking a boat cruise to admire the peninsula's beauty from the sea.

Combine birding with brunch along a repurposed railway

 Connection with nature, walking trails, migratory visitors

 March to May & September to November

USA

Though its name nods to a more industrial past, Atlanta's BeltLine is an unlikely, unexpected and underrated urban birding oasis. Known as the 'emerald necklace around the city', this sprawling green space marries abundant nature-scapes, vistas and that ruddy Georgia clay with easy accessibility to Atlanta's vibrant centre. On forest-fringed sections of the route, there are plenty of opportunities for spotting a true variety of birdlife – from red-shouldered hawks swirling in the sky above to brown thrashers flitting through the treeline or titmice faffing about in leaf litter. And there's something to see at every turn: even along more urban sections, you might catch Halloween-hued Baltimore orioles building hanging nests in the boughs of American elms, which are also the preferred smorgasbord spot of the small purple finch.

Still a work in progress, the BeltLine's 30-plus miles (48km) of pathways – mostly former railway tracks repurposed as multiuse trails – connect reservoirs, city parks and woodlands, where soil regeneration projects and the planting of trees and shrubs (almost all native to the region) have increased the bounty and diversity of birdlife. It's not quite a tourist highlight, and the BeltLine's location – running smack-dab through the middle of some of Atlanta's most bustling neighbourhoods and business districts – means that it may not be top of mind for birders, but it absolutely should be.

Style, substance, swifts & sustainability
Along the Eastside and

Right: The bright plumage of a male Baltimore oriole

Below: Atlanta's BeltLine loops around the city, offering plenty of access points on foot or bicycle

© Drone Stock Pros / Shutterstock; Al Mueller / Shutterstock; Courtesy of Tenijah Hamilton

Q&A

What's a can't-miss BeltLine locale?
If there's a Venn diagram where one circle says food and the other says birds, where they overlap is my own personal nirvana – I like to go where those two things meet. There's a really cool outdoor eatery called Ladybird on the Eastside Trail, and you can often find me there – burger in one hand, binoculars in the other!

If you skip the BeltLine you're missing out on...
Walking or biking between all the different habitats! You have lots of wooded areas, then some grasslands where the sparrows hide. You can hit the Historic Fourth Ward Park just off the Eastside Trail – I love seeing the ruby-crowned kinglets there and there's a pond so you get to see some awesome ducks. Basically, you DON'T want to miss this.

Sheridan Alford, Birds Georgia director of community engagement

Left: You can even birdwatch with a beer at New Realm

Right: Listen for birds in the woodland of Davidson-Arabia Mountain Nature Preserve

via the Gulf of Mexico, to the US South and onwards from there. Looking deceptively like avant-garde installations, the towers bring conservation to the forefront, piquing the curiosity of the scores of people who walk, jog, bike and blade past them every day.

Not either/or, but both

We're often told that we need to escape city life and retreat to the 'great outdoors', but along these pathways it is easy to be reminded that the natural world is not a place we run away to, but that nature should be, could be and ultimately is wherever we are.

The BeltLine is not so much an intrusion on city life as an invitation to see the natural world for what it actually is: inextricably linked to us, from ravines to restaurants, nests to neighbourhoods, from our daily commute right down to the core of our communities.

Don't Miss

→ Spotting eastern bluebird nestlings in the Eastside's Piedmont Park

→ Soaking up indigo bunting serenades at the Westside Park quarry

→ Brewery birding at the BeltLine's New Realm while sipping an Ascot Owl ale

Westside Trails, keep an eye out for altars to the city's part-time residents, cigar-shaped chimney swifts. Nestled in gardens of insect-attracting plants like bee balm, these mural-covered, 24ft (7m)-high towers provide respite for the swifts, which feed on the wing but have suffered from declining food sources. Engineered to suit the particular aerodynamics of chimney swift anatomy, the towers serve as roosting spots where the birds can rest, recharge and repopulate during their long journey from South America,

Find Your Joy

Getting there
The Eastside Trail is around 30 minutes by rideshare or car/taxi from Atlanta's Hartsfield–Jackson

Airport. Given its central location, the BeltLine is easily accessible by public transport; plan bus, train or streetcar routes on the MARTA website (www.itsmarta.com). Close to the Eastside Trail, Krog Street Market is a good place to fuel up before hitting the BeltLine at Irwin St.

Accessibility
The BeltLine's paved paths are accessible to wheelchairs and other mobility aids.

When to go
The BeltLine blooms in spring (March to May), when birds flock in to feed on the new growth. September to October offer a crisper respite to the summer heat, and the

possibility of catching starling murmurations.

Further information
· Free to visitors.
· Open year-round.
· No specialist facilities.
· BeltLine trails host multiple food and drink venues.
· Stay at the nearby Hotel Clermont, an Atlanta institution.
· www.beltline.org

© Iris van den Broek / Shutterstock; Carmen K. Sisson/Cloudybright / Alamy Stock Photo

Other Atlanta Birding Sites

Centennial Olympic Park

Right in the heart of downtown Atlanta, and a legacy of the 1996 Olympic Games, the Centennial is a popular playground and gathering spot and has also become something of an attraction for birds, warblers in particular. Known as a 'habitat island', this green oasis offers food and shelter to migratory species against a backdrop of skyscrapers and traffic.

Don't Miss
Spotting migrating mourning and blackpoll warblers, usually rare in the region.

Davidson-Arabia Mountain Nature Preserve, Stonecrest

A 20-minute drive east of Atlanta, this 62-sq-mile (162-sq-km) national heritage area features wetlands, pine forests and lakes, as well as granite so remarkable it was used to make the Brooklyn Bridge. Hikes might reveal sightings of cedar waxwings, brown-headed nuthatches and white-eyed vireos; keep an eye out for forthcoming bird habitat projects along the South River.

Don't Miss
Geocaching on the Klondike Trail, a moderate 4 mile (6km) loop.

Hang out with gentoo penguins on the White Continent

 Endemic species, engaging your senses, wonder

 November to March

ANTARCTICA

A pungent whiff of guano carries on the icy breeze, and 15,000 gentoo penguins are honking like party horns – you've arrived in Antarctica, and as day dawns bright on Cuverville Island, the light bouncing off snowy shores, stained-glass-blue waters and dark fangs of rock is so dazzling you have to shield your eyes.

When the engines of zodiac dinghies shuttling in visitors are switched off, silence is usually total in Antarctica but for the distant boom of a glacier, the chink of an iceberg or the blow of a whale. But not on Cuverville: gentoo penguins are noisy little dudes, and this is one of Antarctica's biggest colonies, with more than 7000 breeding pairs.

Here the gentoos are on to a good thing: this tiny speck in the Errera Channel, squished between Rongé Island and Graham Land, is mostly icecap, but its north coast is scalloped with the broad, rocky, cliff-rimmed bays that they love for nesting. In the shallows, you'll see gentoos porpoising at speed – their webbed feet make them the fastest swimmers of all penguins, reaching underwater speeds of 30mph (48km/h) .

Suits you, gentoo

No matter how many nature docs you binge-watch or travel mags you read, you can never prepare for the reality of Antarctica. After two days of crossing the storm-smashed Drake Passage, you emerge into calm waters and another world entirely – one barely touched by human hand, where the wildlife is just there. So too with the Cuverville gentoos: slip out of the zodiac and there's your welcome committee.

Right: Gentoo penguins have distinctive white markings on their heads

Below: A gentoo penguin nesting ground on Cuverville Island

© PhotoStock-Israel / Alamy Stock Photo; nwdph / Shutterstock; Tasfoto / Alamy Stock Photo

Q&A

Why do gentoos love Cuverville?
The island's rocky slopes give gentoos a place to build nests on solid ground, with easy access to krill-rich waters just offshore. The slopes are traversed by 'penguin highways', and visitors should remember that penguins always have right of way.

What's so special about gentoos?
Gentoos are doting parents with a gentle demeanour, and are relatively adaptable. They lay eggs earlier or later depending on seasonal conditions. The best time to see fluffy chicks is January to mid-February.

Any funny gentoo tales to share?
While conducting a Cuverville penguin survey, I watched a gentoo steal over a dozen pebbles from its neighbour's nest. The thief would wait until its neighbour looked the other way, then lean over to pilfer a rock. Suddenly, the victimised neighbour let loose a high-pressure stream of guano, right in the face of the thief!

Noah Strycker, writer, photographer & onboard ornithologist

According to conservation guidelines, penguin-watchers should keep a 17ft (5m) distance. But friendly, naturally curious gentoos didn't get the memo and will often come right up to you, sliding belly first or waddling across the snow for a tug at your boots or bag straps. Gentoos are usually slick-feathered and stylish, with white-striped heads and red-orange bills, but come February or March you'll see some having a bad hair day, looking like exploding pillows as they go through their annual catastrophic moult.

Right: Peril for penguins; the leopard seal

Far right: Chinstrap penguins in the South Shetland Islands

Rising rock stars

Gentoos are the nest-proud rookery builders of the penguin world. Males woo potential mates with gifts of pebbles and build circular nests from them; fights for the best stones can turn nasty. Family matters to these nurturing penguins, who are monogamous and form lasting bonds with their chicks. Gentoos are the rock stars here, but you might also sight other birdlife, from Antarctic shags to skuas and storm-petrels. Predators are thankfully few, though hefty leopard seals who like to snack on penguins, lurk offshore.

Ironically, climate change has worked in the gentoos' favour. Their status on the IUCN Red List has gone from 'near threatened' to 'least concern' in recent years: as melting sea ice and warmer waters have freed up new breeding areas, the penguins' numbers have been steadily increasing.

Don't Miss

→ **Seeing pebble-carrying gentoo penguins scoot across the snow**

→ **Marvelling at gentoos porpoising next to your zodiac**

→ **Hearing gentoos honk as day breaks over Antarctica**

Find Your Joy

Getting there
Tour specialists like Swoop Antarctica (www.swoop-antarctica.com) help with logistics: choosing itineraries and cabins, booking flights and transport. Most expedition voyages depart from Ushuaia, Argentina. Aerolíneas Argentinas operate direct flights between Buenos Aires or El Calafate and Ushuaia. A 10-night expedition in a shared cabin typically costs around £6000. Book well in advance. Some cruises provide cold-weather gear; many have onboard experts (and ornithologists).

Accessibility
Cruise lines like Holland America (www.hollandamerica.com) have wheelchair-accessible rooms. But the voyage demands a good level of fitness – the storms, bitter cold and seasickness can be challenging.

When to go
Peak season coincides with the melting pack ice (roughly November to March). Go in late January or February to see penguin chicks; February and March are best for whale- and seal-watching.

Further information
• Access via organised cruises only.

Other Antarctica Penguin Hot-spots

Snow Hill Island

Glimpsing a mighty emperor penguin is a pinch-yourself moment. These tallest and heaviest of all penguins breed and raise chicks on the ice at Snow Hill Island, off the Antarctic Peninsula's east coast in the Weddell Sea. This Important Bird Area is the world's northernmost emperor penguin rookery, home to a 10,000-strong colony. Getting here involves a polar ship, helicopter and icy trek.

Don't miss

The emperor penguins' entrancing courtship displays, where they turn and bow deeply to each other.

Half Moon Island

Forming a perfect crescent at the entrance to Moon Bay in the South Shetland Islands, this craggy, snow-polished, savagely beautiful island harbours a colony of 3300 breeding pairs of dapper chinstrap penguins, with their black 'tuxedos' and distinctive helmet-like markings. Observe them socialising, sledging and going about their business among the rocky turrets and spires.

Don't miss

Seeing chinstrap penguins waddling and rock-hopping across the pebble bay.

© robertharding / Alamy Stock Photo

Asia

Watch red-crowned cranes dance in Hokkaidō

 Endemic species, appreciation of beauty, rural landscapes

 November to March

JAPAN

Temperatures around Akan town, on Japan's main northern island of Hokkaidō, can dip to -15°C (5°F) in winter. The snow lies thick on the ground and the pine trees sparkle, their needles frosted with ice. But every morning, at around 7.30am, all thoughts of the cold evaporate as eyes turn skyward to view the flock of red-crowned cranes – up to 150 strong – flying overhead. The birds land gracefully in the field beside the Akan International Crane Center in southeastern Hokkaidō to feed on corn kernels that have been scattered on the snow.

Named for its signature crimson forehead, the red-crowned crane, or tancho, is the most striking of Japan's three commonly seen crane species. These majestic, spindly-legged birds average 5ft (1.5m) in height and have a wingspan of up to 8ft (2.4m). Because of the lifelong bond between mating couples, the tancho is a beloved national symbol of good fortune, longevity and, above all, loyalty.

Dancing for a date

It's the cranes' characteristic 'dance' that brings tens of thousands of visitors to the wilds of northeastern Hokkaidō every year. As the male coos singly, and the female replies with a double coo, the cranes begin their courtship pas de deux by dipping their heads, throwing their heads back and then bowing again. The sinuous movements of these long-necked birds are quite mesmerising. Then both cranes spread their wings and bounce up and down around each other, as if they're jitterbugging. It's impossible not to be charmed.

Cranes carry out this bonding

Right: Adult red-crowned cranes have a wingspan of 6–8ft (1.8–2.4m)

Below: The choreographed courtship dance of Hokkaidō's red-crowned cranes

Q&A

Do cranes really mate for life?
They may change partners, if injury or illness prevents them having offspring. But I was greatly moved by the bond between a pair of cranes who used to visit the centre – they stayed together even though one could no longer fly.

Top tip for photographing cranes?
Learn about their behaviour, so you can anticipate their actions. By knowing this and having your camera ready, you can take wonderful photos.

Any funny stories about cranes?
When the female is ready to mate, she spreads her wings and the male attempts to mount her. If the male mistimes this manoeuvre, the female can get angry and even attack the male. The expressions of the embarrassed male and the furious female can be quite comical.

Miyuki Kawase, Akan International Crane Center director

© AndreAnita / Shutterstock; Pichit Tongma / Shutterstock; Various images / Shutterstock

Left: Hokkaidō's red-crowned cranes live on the island year-round

Right: Marvel at migrating whooping cranes in Canada

cranes on his land during winter, and began to provide food to help them survive the cold season. Others followed suit and the crane population began slowly but steadily to recover

Established in 1996, the Akan International Crane Center specialises in researching and conserving Japanese cranes, with an exhibition room where visitors can learn about the birds' behaviour and ecology. Though it remains an official feeding station, the centre is also engaged in efforts to reduce human feeding by pumping water to a pond to increase aquatic life year-round, so creating an environment where red-crowned cranes can feed naturally. Fireflies now breed around the pond in the summer, when the centre also organises firefly-viewing events. Hopefully, all this work will result in future generations continuing to be charmed by the synchronised dance moves of the tancho.

Don't Miss

→ **Enjoying the dips and jumps of the cranes' courtship dance**

→ **Exploring the wide open spaces of Hokkaidō**

→ **Spotting tancho year-round in nearby Kushiro Shitsugen National Park**

ritual year-round, but it's most easily observed in Hokkaidō during the long winter at two locations – the Akan International Crane Center, and the Tsurui-Ito Tancho Sanctuary – where food is provided for the approximately 1900 wild cranes that live and breed in the island's wetlands.

Caring for cranes
The roots of this human intervention programme date back some 70 years, to a time when wild tancho were in grave danger of extinction. In 1950, Akan farmer Yamazaki Sadajiro noticed

Find Your Joy

Getting there
From New Chitose Airport, Hokkaidō's air hub, it's a 3½-hour drive or a four-hour train

journey to Kushiro, the closest town to the Akan International Crane Center. From JR Kushiro train station, take a bus to the Tancho-no-Sato bus stop, a journey of about an hour; the Crane Center is then a 5-minute walk.

Accessibility
There's step-free access to the Akan International Crane Center, but some exhibition areas are not wheelchair accessible. Support is offered for those who need assistance.

When to go
From November to early March, to make up for the lack of food for the birds in the wild, feeding is carried out at the Akan International Crane Center at 8am and 1pm. At peak times, about 150 red-crowned cranes fly in and perform their beautiful dance.

Further information
• Admission charge.
• Open year-round.
• Observation room at Akan Crane Center.
• Cafe on site.
• Accommodation nearby in Kushiro.
• https://aiccgrus.wixsite.com/aiccgrus

© IamDoctorEgg / Shutterstock; John L Absher / Shutterstock

Other Places to See Cranes

Wood Buffalo National Park, Canada

Bring your binoculars and look to the skies over this World Heritage Site, straddling the borders of Alberta and the Northwest Territories. A remote area of this vast park is the breeding ground of the last wild migratory flock of whooping cranes in the world, and sighting them swooping overhead is an unforgettable thrill.

Don't miss
The snowy white plumage, crimson cap and bugling call of the tallest bird in North America.

Hornborgasjön, Sweden

Every year, from mid-March to mid-April, bird lovers converge to watch some 19,500 common cranes gather at this 11-sq-mile (28-sq-km) lake, around two hours' drive northeast of Gothenburg. The cranes pause here to feed on the huge piles of grain that are spread beside the lake to help them refuel on their long journeys from Spain and Germany to breeding grounds in Europe's far north.

Don't miss
The courting cranes' mesmerising dance moves.

Marvel at hornbills swooping above the jungle

 Rare encounters, awe, engaging your senses

 January to April

Morning light filters through tangled jungle and mist rises in wisps from the emerald-green mountains of Khao Yai National Park. Daybreak ruffles feathers, and birds are going about the noisy business of breakfast. As the sun rises in a perfect golden orb, the trees pulse and thrum with life.

Cackles, hoots, warbles, trills, whoops and caws reverberate through dry evergreen, montane mixed deciduous and tropical rainforest – like morning mantras offered in this temple to the green gods. Elephants sway through the grasslands, pounding trails flat as they make their thirsty way to a watering hole. 'Beware Tigers' signs mark bends on the roads snaking through the park, though some say the tigers are long gone.

Suddenly, there's a flash of brilliant yellow high in a fig tree, and a low rumble like a chainsaw cranking up echoes through the jungle. You train your binoculars on a great hornbill – the most magnificently odd-looking of birds, with its dramatically curved yellow bill, weighty casque and beautiful black-and-white plumage. With breath held and heart racing, you watch in silent wonder as it preens its feathers, catches the morning sun in the high branches and casually nibbles on figs. Then, just as abruptly, it takes flight, swooping with effortless grace above the canopy, as unmissable as a glider plane, with a wingspan of up to 6ft (1.8m).

Right: Spotting hornbills in Khao Yai National Park

Below: A great hornbill in Khao Yai National Park

© Pisaisit Watcharotai / Shutterstock; vanchai / Shutterstock; soft_light / Shutterstock; kajornyot wildlife photography / Shutterstock

Q&A

Best time to see Khao Yai's hornbills?
From December to March, skies are clear, bird activity is high and the great hornbills disappear into the canopy of fruiting fig trees. The best time to see the shy, seldom-seen Austin's brown hornbill is from March to June when they are breeding.

Key places to spot them?
The oriental pied hornbill can frequently be found in the campsites, where they often gather in the late afternoon before going to roost. Local guides know where fruiting trees are, making Khao Yai one of the easiest places in Asia to see hornbills.

How do you tell them apart?
All four species differ in size and plumage, with distinctive calls easily recognised once the sounds are pointed out. Interestingly, the sound of the wing beats of the largest two species, great and wreathed hornbills, can be distinguished – they probably use this sound as some sort of territorial or communication device.

Nick Upton, Thailand-based birding expert and private guide

Thailand's wild side

A vast expanse of shocking green, Unesco World Heritage-listed Khao Yai, 124 miles (200km) north of Bangkok, is Thailand's oldest and third-largest national park. And what a beauty it is. These cool mountains, dense forests, plunging falls and open grasslands are a birder's dream. Of all the 280-odd bird species here, the real prize is the chance to spot four varieties of hornbill.

During the January to April breeding season, hornbills turn up the volume, becoming increasingly vocal, with guttural barks, growls and roars as they go all out to attract a mate. Males and females perform duets up in the park's mature fruit trees – listen for the 'kok' and rumble of the great hornbill, the squeaky-toy chuckle of the oriental pied hornbill, the 'uk-uk-uk' of the smaller wreathed hornbill, and the piercing 'waew-waew' of the rare, orange-brown feathered Austen's brown hornbill.

Right: Haew Suwat waterfall in Khao Yai National Park

Far right: A Malabar pied hornbill feasting on fruit

Hit the trails

Get lucky and you'll glimpse a hornbill from a park lay-by or watchtower, but hiking one of the trails – with or without guide – really ups your chances of a sighting. Top billing goes to Trail 2, which twists for 2 miles (3km) from Pa Gluay Mai Campsite to Haew Suwat waterfall. The scenery is the full-on *Jungle Book* fantasy, with babbling streams, crashing falls and unruly gibbons swinging from tree to tree. Listen carefully and study the canopy and you might well snatch a glimpse of all four hornbill species.

Don't Miss

→ **Listening to the sunrise concert of birds**

→ **Scanning the sky to spy a great hornbill in flight**

→ **Catching the breeding season duets and casque-butting**

Find Your Joy

Getting there
Hiring a car gives greater flexibility. By public transport from Bangkok, take a train, coach or private minivan to Pak Chong, then a songthaew bus to Chao Por Khao Yai Shrine Visitor Centre.

Accessibility
Trails can be rough underfoot, hard to follow and overgrown, making Khao Yai a challenge for those with mobility issues.

When to go
Prime time for hornbills in Khao Yai is from January to April, when you can observe their breeding rituals, but there's good birding until the monsoon rains sweep in (the quiet, rainy season is from June to September). Avoid weekends and public holidays when the park gets overcrowded. Allow at least three days for the best chance of spotting hornbills.

Further information
• Admission charge.
• Open year-round.
• Wildlife lookouts and watchtower.
• Cafe and restaurant on-site.
• Camping and lodges are available at the park (booking highly advisable).
• www. khaoyainationalpark. com

Other Hornbill Hot-spots

Dandeli Wildlife Sanctuary, India

In the southwestern state of Karnataka, Dandeli's lush, trail-woven forests teem with creatures great and small – from monkeys, elephants and tigers to some 270 species of bird. Among them are nine species of hornbill, including Malabar pied hornbills and Indian grey hornbills. Prime hornbill season runs from October to May. Kali Adventure Camp is a great springboard for exploring, with birdwatching walks and jungle-immersed lodges.

Don't miss

February's Hornbill Festival sees guided hikes and activities revolving around these incredible birds.

Sumatra, Indonesia

Smouldering volcanoes and thick, glossy rainforest make the ruggedly beautiful island of Sumatra ripe for eco adventure. Jungle trekkers gravitate towards the vast old-growth forests of the spectacularly biodiverse Gunung Leuser National Park in the island's north, which also delivers some of the world's most sensational hornbill spotting.

Don't miss

Peering up into ancient trees to glimpse the wondrous rhinoceros hornbill, a slick black-feathered number with an orange-red bill and casque.

Days out with the dancers of paradise

 Courtship displays, endemic birds, pristine reefs

 October to April

INDONESIA

Although it's still dark, the moon casts enough of a milky glow onto these warm turquoise seas that the boat driver doesn't need a torch to steer a course. Instead, the light of the moon guides the vessel to a gentle halt on a beach dusted with sand the colour and texture of sugar. Grabbing a pair of binoculars, the guide leads the way off the beach, under swaying coconut palms into the tangled, jungle-draped interior of a small tropical island that is home to that prince of the avian world, the bird-of-paradise.

This is the experience waiting in the Raja Ampat archipelago, a remote gathering of 1500 islands and coral outcrops in eastern Indonesia. Until recently, Raja Ampat was a place few had heard of, but then adventurous scuba divers discovered that the islands were fringed with pristine coral reefs, housing such an explosive diversity of marine life that the archipelago quickly gained a reputation as one of the world's best diving locations. And that's not all...

Show-dancers of the bird world
It's not only carnival-coloured fish that call these paradise islands home. There are also myriad birds, some of them every bit as flamboyant as the fish on the reefs. Raja Ampat is home to two endemic species of the appropriately named bird-of-paradise – the red bird-of-paradise and the Wilson's bird-of-paradise – as

Right: A male Wilson's bird-of-paradise performing a courtship display on Raja Ampat

Below: A red bird-of-paradise practising in his treetop lek on Raja Ampat

© Rich Carey / Shutterstock; Nature Picture Library / Alamy Stock Photo; Gabbro / Alamy Stock Photo; Matt Munro / Lonely Planet

Q&A

There are quite a few species of bird-of-paradise, aren't there?
Yes, there are 45 found all over the island of New Guinea.

Are birdwatchers the only ones to appreciate their beauty?
In the past – and it's probably still happening today – people would capture these birds for their feathers. They were used in the headdresses of some tribes in New Guinea and by women in Europe to decorate their hats when they went to balls.

And are they under threat today?
The population is stable, especially in those areas where tourists come to see the birds, because the locals have understood the value of these birds alive in their natural habitat. This, unfortunately, does not mean that trapping and hunting these amazing creatures is nonexistent, but there's less of it.

Mehd Halaouate, Papua birding guide

Left: The limestone island outcrops of Raja Ampat

Right: A Raggiana bird-of-paradise performs to a female in Varirata National Park

Don't Miss

→ Marvelling at the intricate dance moves of a male bird-of-paradise

→ Seeing both of Raja Ampat's endemic bird-of-paradise species

→ Mixing up birding with dives to see sharks and manta rays

well as several non-endemic birds-of-paradise.

On a bird-of-paradise tour of the island's steamy interior, your guide will lead you up from the beach through the heat and humidity of the tangled jungle to a clearing in the forest, then silently motion for you to settle down and wait. The moon will slip below the horizon and with the first rays of daylight, the dancers of paradise will be ready to put on a show.

A feathered extravaganza

Flying in from the left, a male red bird-of-paradise lands on the dead branch of a tree and readies himself. At first there's a mere wiggle of the body, as if he is tuning in to a musical beat that human observers are unaware of. Satisfied, he opens his wings and begins to vibrate them furiously. Then his entire body starts shaking and he spins around and around. Long, party-streamer-like tailfeathers add extra razzmatazz to the performance as he lets rip with a strong, high-pitched song.

Shortly afterwards, a female lands on a nearby branch and the male pirouettes with ever increasing intensity. For a few moments the tree becomes a kaleidoscope of rotating red feathers. But then, tragedy! Unimpressed, the female turns her back and flies off in search of a better partner. Don't worry, however: there'll be more chances to see champion dancers on a trip to the islands of paradise!

Find Your Joy

Getting there
From Jakarta, fly to Sorong in West Papua and take a public ferry to the main Raja Ampat island of Waisai. Much of the accommodation is on smaller offshore islands; guesthouse owners and diving lodges will collect you by boat from Waisai.

Accessibility
Jungle paths are slippery and uneven, and you'll need to climb into and out of boats, so this isn't an easy option for travellers with disabilities.

When to go
Birds-of-paradise are visible all year but the dry season (October to April) is when the birds are easiest to see and the islands are easier to travel around, due to drier weather conditions and calmer seas.

Further information
• Admission charge.
• Open year-round.

• Birdwatching guides can be arranged through most of the diving lodges.
• Birding tours typically include meals.
• Resorts aimed at divers can be found throughout the archipelago.

© attiandt / Getty Images; feathercollector / Shutterstock

Other Carnivalesque Birds

Varirata National Park, Papua New Guinea

Only an hour's drive from Papua New Guinea's capital, Port Moresby, forested Varirata National Park is perhaps the easiest place in the world to see birds-of-paradise. Easy walking trails lead to observation points where you can spy the spectacular Raggiana bird-of-paradise – symbol of Papua New Guinea – and four other bird-of-paradise species.

Don't miss
Keeping your eyes peeled for the prehistoric-looking dwarf cassowary.

Papua's Arfak Mountains, Indonesia

Never mind Norman Foster and Frank Gehry – the world's best architect is actually the bower bird. Creating fortress-like nests on the ground and decorating them with colourful found objects that recall a carnival float, these extraordinary birds can be spotted in the thick forests of Papua's Arfak Mountains. Hides have been set up in key places, and quality guides are on hand.

Don't miss
Witnessing the extraordinary 'spinning top' dance of the western parotia, another Papuan bird-of-paradise.

Make like a maharaja in peacock-filled palace grounds

♡ Vivid colours, history, breathing space

🕐 November to March

INDIA

If you've ever dreamed of being a king or queen for a day, the sprawling Falaknuma Palace – former home of the Nizam of Hyderabad, once the world's richest man – will give you a taste of the indulgent lifestyle enjoyed by India's maharajas. It's only appropriate, then, that the palace's elegant grounds provide a home for that self-styled king of birds, the preening peacock.

Today, the Falaknuma is a lavish hotel dripping with statuary and stained glass, but the real drama takes place in the grounds, where peacocks display flamboyantly along tracks navigated by horse-drawn coaches. Step out at dawn or dusk and you'll be bombarded by an operatic overture, with the mournful call of peacocks answering the call to prayer from the medieval mosques of old Hyderabad.

Nature's dandies

If any bird is a better metaphor for the lives of the world's most privileged princes, we've yet to find it. Peacocks are pumped-up popinjays, to borrow a parrot metaphor – disdainfully aware that Mother Nature has gifted them a rainbow raiment to make other birds green (and blue) with envy. Add in a bumper serving of pride, a sprinkling of arrogance, a hint of pomposity and a supersized serving of vanity, and you've got the perfect pet for the maharaja who has everything.

At the Falaknuma, you don't just get one ornamental fowl wandering the grounds – you get a profusion. The palace flock of more than 100 peacocks and peahens is fed daily

Right: The larger the tail, the more appealing the male peacock

Below: Falaknuma Palace, the name means 'mirror of the sky' in Urdu

My Birding Joy

It's hard to concentrate on your sun salutations with an amorous peacock doing its best to distract you, but that's an occupational hazard when you sign up for a morning yoga class at the Falaknuma Palace.

For my part, I didn't mind. As soon as the class was over, I changed out of my hotel-supplied white pyjamas, grabbed my camera and spent several happy hours wandering through the palace's elegant grounds, snapping peacocks performing their extravagant displays and soaking up the views over the rooftops of old Hyderabad.

And there were peacocks and peahens everywhere! As I strolled between the palace pavilions, they stalked the lawns, strutted out of the bushes and took short, clumsy flights from the balustrades. Sure, it wasn't an out-in-the-wild birding adventure, but it remains one of my most memorable avian encounters.

Joe Bindloss

© photomaster / Shutterstock; Jan Willem van Hofwegen /Shutterstock; Sokolik Nat 77 / Shutterstock

at 5.30pm, but for the rest of the day, the birds run wild in the grounds. You'll spy them lolling under topiary, strutting around the ornamental ponds, launching into bumbling flights from the crenelated palace walls and shaking a tailfeather in one of the most uplifting courtship displays in the avian world.

Right: A statue at Falaknuma overlooks Hyderabad

Far right: Udaipur's Lake Palace on Lake Pichola

Lavish displays of love

While some guests relax in rose-petal baths, those with a birding bent wander gardens dotted with wedding-cake pavilions, spotting painted peacocks and their dressed-down spouses emerging from every patch of undergrowth. Indeed, these primped-up pheasants are so preoccupied by courtship that they hardly seem to notice human spectators.

The most atmospheric time to admire the palace peacocks is at first light – stake out a calm vantage point and watch the theatre unfold. Peacocks may be unrepentantly arrogant, but the transformation as trailing display feathers flick up to become a quivering canopy adorned with hundreds of bottle-green eyes is an expression of pure joy.

There's every chance you'll find the odd eye-feather blowing around in the palace grounds. Don't balk at picking it up – in Indian mythology, the peacock is associated with Lakshmi, the Hindu goddess of wealth and good fortune, and prosperity is believed to follow when peacock feathers are brought into the home.

Don't Miss

→ Catching a peacock in full display mode in the palace grounds

→ The peacocks' haunting call floating in the early morning mist

→ Retreating for high tea on the Falaknuma's Jade Terrace

Find Your Joy

Getting there
The Falaknuma crowns a hill to the south of old Hyderabad; most guests arrive by taxi or chartered car. If you can't stretch to the hefty room rates, visit on a guided tour with Telangana Tourism (https://telanganatourism.org.in).

Accessibility
As the Falaknuma was built in the 1880s, its grounds and interiors feature steep steps and slopes, but peacocks can be seen from the level main driveways.

When to go
Come from November to March for dry days and warm, not baking, temperatures; from April to May, it can be too hot for comfort. Avoid the damp monsoon months from June to September.

Further information
• Free to guests; fee for guided tours.
• Year-round.
• No specialist facilities.
• The Falaknuma's restaurants include Adaa and Gol Bungalow; old Hyderabad has many less pricey options.
• Hyderabad has all-budget alternatives to the Falaknuma's upscale rooms.
• www.tajhotels.com

© Jan Willem van Hofwegen / Shutterstock; Pete Seaward / Lonely Planet

Other Indian Birding Palaces

Taj Lake Palace, Udaipur

In the marble palaces of Rajasthan's White City, the birdlife comes to you. From the terrace of the Taj Lake Palace hotel – made famous by the Bond film *Octopussy* – you'll see the likes of tufted ducks, black-headed ibis and oriental darters frolicking on the silvery waters of Lake Pichola. In fact, with every room featuring a lake view, you don't even need to get out of bed.

Don't miss

Flocks of birds taking flight over the gleaming lake at sunset.

Laxmi Vilas Palace Hotel, Bharatpur

You'll have to step outside the elegant, fresco-adorned walls of this 19th-century palace east of Jaipur for the best birding experiences, but you're just minutes from the waterfowl-filled wetlands of Keoladeo National Park, a vital rest stop for some 370 bird species, including migrating cranes, spoonbills, storks, pelicans and eagles.

Don't miss

The sudden influx of migratory visitors each October.

See kingfishers among the stupas in Sri Lanka's first capital

 Serenity, connecting with nature, ancient history

 January to March

SRI LANKA

If you ever feel despondent about humans encroaching on nature, remember that nature can encroach back. Among the pilgrim-thronged stupas of Anuradhapura, Sri Lanka's first capital, forgotten, tumbled temples spill from the forests, empty and...well, not quite silent, as birds of every size, shape and colour flit from lintel to column to carving.

Away from the famous-name dagobas, this depopulated metropolis – home at one time to two million souls – has been reclaimed as a playground for birdlife and a prime fishing ground for six species of kingfishers, which dart like animated jewels between the stupas, shrines and temple pillars.

Anuradhapura's avian roll call
Anuradhapura attracts a varied wealth of birds, from stocky hawk-eagles and fishing eagles to theatrical hoopoes, noisy scops owls, sapphire-bright bee-eaters, sunshine-yellow orioles, even-more-vivid-than-the-name-suggests blue magpies and rambunctious pied hornbills, often heard clattering in the trees at sunset.

But even in this esteemed company, kingfishers stand out for their personality, grace and poise. The gasp-inducing moment when a kingfisher plunges from its waterside perch like a lethal dart and emerges with a speared fish balanced in its beak – but barely a bead of moisture on its brilliantine feathers – is an experience to treasure.

A profusion of kingfishers
At Anuradhapura, kingfishers come common, pied, three-toed (oriental dwarf), stork-billed, white-throated and blue-eared,

Right: The Ruwanweli Maha Seya stupa at Anuradhapura

Below: A white-throated kingfisher at Anuradhapura

© ra.photo / Shutterstock; Guillaume.B / Shutterstock; Lubos Houska / Shutterstock

Q&A

What makes Anuradhapura good for birding?
Anuradhapura is known as the 'kingdom of water reservoirs', with water tanks, paddy fields and forests that attract many birds, plus ancient ruins and temples that create a paradise for bird lovers. It's a great site for birders travelling with a non-birding partner.

Any tips for spotting kingfishers?
Normally kingfishers are active all day. Look for them perched on branches, fences and phone lines beside ponds and tanks. The three-toed (oriental dwarf) kingfisher is a little gem. Very colourful and hard to see.

What other birds should people look out for at Anuradhapura?
A long list! Black drongos, racket-tailed drongos, Malabar pied hornbills, Sri Lanka grey hornbills, Sri Lanka woodshrikes, paradise flycatchers, golden-backed woodpeckers, grey-headed and white-bellied fish eagles...

Prasanjith Caldera, Walk With Jith Tours & Travels guide/director

Left: A blue-eared kingfisher dives for a fish

Right: A pheasant-tailed jacana skips across lily pads at Bundala National Park

Finding the fishers

Keep your camera ready – seeing common fishers is almost a given, and the odds are good for stork-billed kingfishers, white-throated kingfishers and the unexpectedly monochrome pied kingfisher. If you glimpse the iridescent blue and purple plumage of the three-toed kingfisher, the brilliant-blue speckles of the blue-eared kingfisher or the dark cowl of the rare black-capped kingfisher, you've been blessed.

Finding kingfishers here is a case of finding water. Ponds and step-ringed sacred tanks pop up everywhere among the dagobas, so rent a bicycle to explore and keep an eye out for that distinctive kingfisher profile.

At the end of an uplifting birding session, reward yourself with a contemplative pause at one of Anuradhapura's sacred stupas. They're at their most magical in the late afternoon, after the human visitors have departed, as roosting birds take over the ruins.

Don't Miss

→ Spotting the jewel-like flash as a kingfisher darts for the water

→ Letting birds lead you to overlooked, ruined temples

→ The few hundred other bird species that frequent the treetops around Anuradhapura

joined on special occasions by visiting black-capped kingfishers from India. But all are master fishers: patient snipers, watching poised and motionless from elevated vantage points beside bodies of water, waiting for the opportune moment to transform pent-up energy into motion.

This gives photographers ample time to snap a perfect kingfisher portrait, though you'll need a long, fast lens and a camera with a rapid burst mode if you hope to capture the precise moment when a fisher breaks the water at the start or end of a hunting foray.

Find Your Joy

Getting there
Sri Lanka's Bandaranaike International Airport is north of Colombo near Negombo; from there, jump on a bus or train to Puttalam and change to a bus bound for Anuradhapura.

Accessibility
Getting deep among the ruins involves navigating uneven pathways, but hiring a car and driver for the day can get you close to Anuradhapura's pools, lakes and tanks, where you can spot to your heart's content.

When to go
June to September sees the clearest skies over Anuradhapura, but temperatures can soar to uncomfortable levels, regularly topping 32°C (90°F). Come from January to March for slightly cooler days and easier sleep at night.

Further information
• Admission charge.
• Year-round.
• Specialist birding guides available.
• Eat among the ruins at the swish Sanctuary at Tissawewa.
• As well as the Sanctuary, Anuradhapura has hotels for all budgets.

© Nattawat Nuanphon / Shutterstock; poylock19 / Shutterstock

Other Top Sri Lankan Birding Spots

Sinharaja Forest Reserve
Sri Lanka's largest lowland rainforest is a garden of Eden for endemic and native birds – and the only way in is on foot, so you're guaranteed to escape the crowds. The pleasure here is basking in untamed nature and the giddy thrill of rare sightings, such as red-faced malkohas, green-billed coucals and Sri Lankan blue magpies. Swing by en route from the south coast to Sri Lanka's emerald tea plantations.

Don't miss
The soundtrack of the forest – joyously free from human-made noise.

Bundala National Park
Preserving a landscape of swamps and tropical lagoons along an unspoiled stretch of Sri Lankan shoreline, Bundala lures birders with 197 recorded species, including migrating greater flamingos, petite blue-tailed bee-eaters, flycatchers, sandpipers and more. You also stand a decent chance of spotting two species of crocodile on birding safaris through the wetlands.

Don't miss
A pink sea of wintering greater flamingos from September to March.

Watch black-necked cranes dance in a Himalayan valley

 Migratory visitors, stunning location, Bhutanese culture

 November to March

BHUTAN

Every year at the end of October, villagers in the remote Himalayan valley of Phobjikha start to cast their eyes expectantly up to the heavens. Within days, as if willed into existence, the first of the season's black-necked cranes appears, circling the golden roofs of the 16th-century Gangte Monastery.

Within weeks the valley resounds with the cries of over 600 cranes (known locally as thrung thrung kam). Phobjikha is not only one of the best places in the world to spot these elegant, long-distance travellers; it's also one of the most dramatic valleys in one of the most remarkable countries on Earth.

Communing with cranes
Spotting cranes in Phobjikha is easy: just follow the Gangte Nature Trail down past ancient Buddhist stupas into the snow-dusted valley. Slowly, the birds start to appear through the frigid morning mist, as they forage on crops and the dwarf bamboo that carpets the marshy valley floor.

With their long black necks and ink-dipped wings, monochrome save for a distinctive red eye-band, the graceful 5ft tall (1.5m) cranes look lifted from a Chinese ink-brush painting. Watching them is a serene, almost meditative experience. With luck, you'll see the birds dance – swooping and leaping with raised wings, as they mark their territory or perform for a prospective mate.

Heavenly visitors
There's a supernatural air to Asia's cranes. Maybe it's their graceful demeanour or their sudden appearance every year, heralding the changing of the seasons; or perhaps it's their inclination

Right: A Gangte Monastery wall painting featuring cranes and the Sage of Long Life

Below: Black-necked cranes are winter visitors from late October to the Phobjikha Valley

© Shakyasom Majumder / Getty Images; Cyrille Redor / Shutterstock; Garden Photo World / Alamy Stock Photo

Q&A

When is the best time to see cranes?
November is a good time, as the weather is not too cold and you can attend the Black-Necked Crane Festival. To witness a large gathering, best come in January but be prepared for the cold. In late February/early March, the courtship dances start.

Do I need to get up early?
Early morning and evening are the best times for spotting, as up to 300 cranes roost together in ponds and their calls echo around the valley.

Where can I find out more?
It's definitely worth visiting Phobjikha's Black-Necked Crane Centre, as it's full of information on cranes and their role in the valley, and your visit supports their conservation. You can use the spotting scopes here in relative warmth and without disturbing the cranes.

Jigme Tshering, Black-Necked Crane Conservation Programme coordinator, Royal Society for Protection of Nature Bhutan

to mate for life, or their literary connections to Tibet's sixth Dalai Lama – but for centuries communities on both sides of the Himalaya have considered the birds auspicious, associated with longevity, prosperity and wisdom. The Bhutanese have a particular respect for these 'heavenly birds', so much so that their arrival is heralded by an annual festival.

Right: Children perform the black-necked crane dance at a festival in Gangte Monastery

Far right: Tso Kar Lake in Ladakh is an important breeding ground for birds

Community connections

Part of the joy in visiting Phobjikha is seeing how harmoniously the local communities cohabit with their avian visitors. Bhutan's famous concept of Gross National Happiness (which essentially means weighing up environmental and cultural considerations alongside economic factors in any decision) has made it natural to shape development around the cranes, instead of the other way around, so power lines have been routed underground to avoid injury to the birds. A flourishing homestay programme offers visitors the chance to explore firsthand how locals perceive the cranes, and gives villagers an important financial stake in the cranes' continued wellbeing.

By the end of winter, the last of the cranes have left the valley on their epic flight back over the Himalaya to the breeding grounds of the Qinghai-Tibetan Plateau. In Phobjikha, the farmers plough their empty fields in preparation for spring, and sing melancholy folk songs lamenting the departure of these remarkable and propitious birds.

Don't Miss

→ Attending the Black-Necked Crane Festival (11 November) at spectacular Gangte Monastery

→ Soaking up valley views while hiking the Gangte Nature Trail

→ Admiring the dives and jumps of a pair of dancing cranes

Find Your Joy

Getting there

All foreign visitors to Bhutan currently have to pay US$100 per person per day to enter the country (discounted from US$200 until 2027), plus charges for a mandatory guide and transportation. Your driver will take you the 45 miles (72km) from Punakha, over the 11024ft (3360m) Lowa La Pass, to reach the high valley at an altitude of 9515ft (2900m).

Accessibility

Phobjikha is not well suited to those with mobility issues, though it is possible to observe cranes through the spotting scopes of the accessible Black-Necked Crane Information Centre.

When to go

November to March is crane season.

Further information

• The Black-Necked Crane Information Centre has a small admission charge, which goes towards crane protection.
• Open year-round.
• Hides available.
• Phobjikha has a good range of homestays, guesthouses and even luxury hotels. All offer food, and there are a couple of simple restaurants.

Other Crane-Spotting Locations

Bumdeling Wildlife Sanctuary

Bhutan's second-most popular place for spotting black-necked cranes is Bumdeling, in the remote and pristine far east. Between November and March, around 70 black-necked cranes (down from 120 two decades ago) overwinter here on the banks of the Kulong Chhu River. The remote location almost guarantees you'll be the only visitor here, apart from the cranes.

Don't miss
Waking up in a village homestay and hiking out through dawn frost to spot roosting cranes.

Tso Kar, India

Tso Kar (the 'White Lake') is one of Ladakh's great high-altitude salt lakes and an important summer nesting ground for many migratory birds, including black-necked cranes. The deep-blue lake is spectacularly framed by snowcapped 19,685ft (6000m) peaks and sits at an elevation of 14,764ft (4500m), so you need to be acclimatised to visit. Tour agencies in Leh can arrange guides and transportation. May to September is the optimum time.

Don't miss
Scanning the magnificent shoreline for cranes and observing their nesting rituals.

Watch hunting eagles on the Bayan-Ölgii steppe

 Rare encounters, cultural heritage, sense of adventure

 September to February

MONGOLIA

A voice comes from inside the *ger*, the yurt-like tent that nomadic Mongolian horse riders and herders call home. The speaker is a Kazakh eagle hunter, dressed in fox and marmot pelts and a yak-wool vest and shouldering a rifle. He has a traditional fur-lined *toortsog* hat pulled down on his head, and on his gauntlet-shielded hand, perched and resplendent, is a Siberian golden eagle with wings raised like a phoenix. The hunt is about to begin.

Lords of the desert

In a country famed for the beauty of its wildernesses, the kingdom of the Berkutchi – the Kazakh eagle hunters of Western Mongolia – is one of the most sublime. As wild as Outback Australia and as extreme as Chile's Atacama Desert, this is a place still largely unknown to the outside world. Here in Bayan-Ölgii – the country's only Muslim/Kazakh-majority province – the airbrushed landscape is smothered by raw skies, empty plains and the eternally snowcapped Altai Mountains. From the minute you arrive, you'll feel you're somewhere completely different to the rest of East Asia.

Within this landscape, the ancient custom of hunting on horseback with highly-trained golden eagles known as berkut – a subspecies of the American golden eagle – has been passed down for thousands of years, chiefly from father to son. But while the hunting is mostly a male domain, the birds of prey are female, taken from their nests before they've learned to fly to create an unbreakable bond with their new masters.

Right: A Kazakh eagle hunter in his *ger*

Below: Mongolia's eagle-hunting festivals are a relatively recent addition

My Birding Joy

Under a pink, alien sky, almost a thousand years after the first hunters started practising their traditional form of falconry on the Eurasian Steppe, I found myself looking over a dusty prairie, in front of an ethnic Kazakh hunter on horseback, with his unflappable golden eagle ready to bring home dinner.

It was a cool spring afternoon in the Altai Mountains and as I looked over the plain, eyed by the eagle, the hunter leapt into action and, with a drawn-out whistle, his raptor soared into the sky.

For an outsider like me, it felt like a transcendent moment, imbued with the spirits of the past. As I squinted into the sun, I saw the eagle spiral, then violently arc downwards like a star dropping from the sky; moments later, she snared a hare in her beak.

Mike MacEacheran

© Vlad Sokolovsky / Shutterstock; Kertu / Shutterstock; takepicsforfun / Shutterstock

Left: A traditional nomadic camp in Altai Tavan Bogd National Park

Right: Bald eagles congregate on Squamish River, Canada, each autumn

Don't Miss

→ Scanning the skyline for a hunting Siberian golden eagle

→ Drinking *arkhi* – a moonshine-like milk vodka – with a Kazakh eagle hunter

→ Appreciating the last vestiges of the nomadic hunting lifestyle

Larger and more fearsome than the males – some say more intelligent, too – the females have fiery maroon napes and a wingspan of up to 28in (72cm); when fully grown, they're capable of spotting prey up to 11 miles (18km) away.

Life on the move

The life of the Kazakh clans has always been a fragile one. Persecuted in their homeland by Soviet-era Communists, many nomadic families today eke out an existence on the bone-dry plains and glaciers of Altai Tavan Bogd National Park, which topple over the Mongolian border into Kazakhstan. Here, as the sun flares at dawn, riders gallop across the steppe as Chinggis Khan once did, with their hunting eagles boomeranging through the air, ever ready to pounce with sharp talons. Foxes and hares are the most common prey, but some birds have the brawn to bring down an adult wolf.

Importantly, the eagles' welfare is paramount to the hunters. There is a hierarchy at play and the birds are lovingly reared and cared for, before being released back into the wild after seven to 10 seasons to breed their own chicks. For centuries, this cycle has continued – but eagle hunting is a dying art, so come to see this sublime spectacle while you can. To watch this union of horse-riding skill and falconry is to witness theatre and tension created almost from thin air.

Find Your Joy

Getting there
Fly from Ulaanbaatar to Ölgii, capital of Bayan-Ölgii Province. Travelling in Western Mongolia is challenging: book a tour (from reputable hotels in Ulaanbaatar or Ölgii) to reach the national park and meet eagle hunters on the steppe.

Accessibility
As most tours involve overnighting on the steppes (often on the floor of a *ger*), and some walking on rough terrain, meeting the eagle hunters can be challenging for those in wheelchairs or with limited mobility. Discuss your needs with your tour operator in advance.

When to go
Eagle hunting peaks in winter (September to February), when snow cover helps birds spot prey, and temperatures range from -20°C to -45°C (-4°F to -49°F); dress appropriately. Ölgii holds three eagle-hunting festivals over September and October (for dates see www.mongolia.travel).

Further information
• National park fee.
• No specialist facilities.
• Hotels and restaurants in Ölgii; tours cover food and accommodation.

© Kirill Skorobogatko / Shutterstock / Shutterstock | Leigh Schumann / Shutterstock

Other Top Places to Spot Eagles

Squamish, Canada

The First Nations settlement of Squamish, 65km (40 miles) north of Vancouver, is often billed as the 'World Eagle Capital'. Thanks to a thronging invasion of spawning coho, chum and pink salmon on the Cheakamus and Squamish Rivers each autumn, the eagles congregate in record numbers from late October through February to talon-grab fish.

Don't miss

Taking a raft trip to spot eagles in their coastal rainforest kingdom.

Moffat, Scotland

Golden eagles are the top predator in the British countryside, and thanks to the South of Scotland Golden Eagle Project, based in the braided Moffat Hills, their numbers are soaring in the Scottish Borders. Translocating and releasing younger raptors has increased the population to over 40 – the highest number here for three centuries. To see the birds for yourself, grab a pair of binoculars, head to the surrounding hills – and be patient.

Don't miss

September's Moffat Golden Eagle Festival.

Seek out masked finfoot on a boat trip through the mangroves

 Peaceful backwaters, endangered species, quirky characters

 Mid-November to mid-February

BANGLADESH

As the early morning mist rises over the still waters of the creek, the elusive finfoot materialises from the shadows of the dense mangrove forest. Furtive and aware of the silent birdwatchers in the nearby boat, she makes her way slowly down to the edge of the muddy creek. Soon afterwards, she is joined by her partner on the shoreline.

The pair pad around on the soft silt, seeking out tasty morsels, supported by luminous green legs and lobed feet specially adapted for the purpose. The male picks up a small crab, washes it, and swallows it whole. Before long they slip away into the maze of watery channels, leaving only their distinctive footprints as a reminder of their presence.

Masked finfoot are rather odd-looking birds, somewhere between a goose and a grebe. The male's chin is black, the female's white; otherwise, they look remarkably similar: brown on the back shading into grey on the neck, with an orangey, carrot-like bill stuck on the end. With around 80 of these rare waterbirds remaining in the vast expanse of the Sundarbans, and a global population of less than 300, spying a finfoot is a once-in-a-lifetime experience.

A flooded forest

The world's largest mangrove forest, the Sundarbans lies at the top of the Bay of Bengal. It spans the border between Bangladesh and India, with two-thirds of it situated within Bangladesh, around the confluence of the Ganges, Brahmaputra and Meghna Rivers. The continuous flow of fresh water exists in delicate balance with the salt

Right: An elusive masked finfoot in the Sundarbans

Below: An aerial view of the Sundarbans mangroves, now a Unesco World Heritage Site

© Sk Hasan Ali / Shutterstock; iqbal.sohag / Shutterstock

Q&A

What sparked your interest in the masked finfoot?
After graduating in 2011, I wanted to understand the current state of our threatened animals. Very little was then known about the masked finfoot in the Sundarbans; it was entirely off the radar of global birding and conservation communities.

Your best finfoot encounter?
Encountering delicate day-old hatchlings: dark grey above, light grey below, they added life to the creek scenery. We saw two chicks with an adult female, foraging in light rain then vanishing into the Sundarbans' grey and green horizon.

What do the Sundarbans mean to you?
Being here is like stepping into the geography of my dreams. Nothing compares. It holds a special place in my heart, not just because it's in my country but due to its uniqueness, complexities, and the stories of love, life and livelihood that it encapsulates.

Sayam U Chowdhury, Bangladeshi conservation biologist

water of the sea, pushed in and pulled out by the rising and falling tides. It's a perfect environment for mangrove trees to flourish – their aerial roots protrude from the multitude of banks created by silt washed down from the Himalayan mountains.

This delicate equilibrium is challenged by the rising water levels caused by climate change, and the inevitable effect of human activity. That said, it is still the most amazing wilderness. Head off along one of the uncountable number of channels and – beyond birdlife – you might not encounter another soul for days (though you may get lucky and catch a glimpse of a Royal Bengal tiger). Stop and listen to the sounds of the forest; lie back in your boat and gaze at the dark sky and the bright stars.

A crown of kingfishers
While the critically endangered

Right: Birders can take houseboats deep into the waterways of the Sundarbans

Far right: Shore birds of Sonadia Island, Bangladesh

masked finfoot is the star of the Sundarbans show, other birds abound, from woodpeckers and owls to eagles and egrets. There is an almost endless supply of kingfishers of all colours and sizes, with the possibility of encountering up to seven species, including the localised brown-winged kingfisher with its blood-red bill. Other fishers come ruddy, black-capped, collared, white-throated, Eurasian and scintillating blue-eared. For birdwatchers, these are halcyon days indeed.

Don't Miss

→ Sighting the masked finfoot along the water's edge

→ Finding fresh Royal Bengal tiger pugmarks glistening in the mud

→ Savouring the Sundarbans' peace and tranquillity, away from the clamour of Dhaka

Find Your Joy

Getting there
Liveaboard boat trips depart from the Bangladeshi port town of Mongla, 26 miles (42km)

south of the city of Khulna and reachable from Dhaka by train (10½ hours), bus (10 hours) or car (7 hours). Book boat trips through local operator Pugmark Tours and Travel (www.pugmarkbd.com), or international outfits like Birdtour Asia (www. birdtourasia.com)

Accessibility
Accessing and moving

around a liveaboard boat will likely be challenging for those with limited mobility. Contact the tour operator directly to discuss any specific requirements.

When to go
While the Sundarbans can be visited at any time of the year, the weather is at its most pleasant from mid-November to mid-February, between the

heat of the summer and the monsoon season.

Further information
• Daily admission charge.
• Guides required for overnight stays, arranged by tour operators.
• Liveaboard trips include meals; bring other supplies with you.

Other Bangladeshi Birding Sites

Karamajal Ranger Station

After several days on a boat, it's a pleasure to stretch your legs along Karamajal's boardwalk. Having heard the haunting two-note call of the mangrove pitta from the boat, you'll finally have a chance to see it here; its green back, buff underside and black 'bandit' mask offset with a flash of iridescent blue in the wing, its red vent bleeding on to its belly.

Don't Miss
Views across the mangrove forest from the observation tower.

Sonadia Island

South of Chittagong, the holiday resort of Cox's Bazar is the starting point for another boat trip, to the coastal mudflats of Sonadia Island. Landing involves taking off your socks and shoes, rolling up your trousers and wading through the silty waters to the shore – all in a quest to see the world's cutest wader, the diminutive spoon-billed sandpiper.

Don't Miss
Watching wheeling flocks of waders along the shoreline.

Europe

© Menno Schaefer / Shutterstock

Eye peregrine falcons in flight between city towers

♡ Urban views, natural grace, high speeds

🕐 July to February

A sketchpad and pencils would be a reasonable thing to take to an art gallery. You could get away with paints and an easel. But unless the artworks are very far away, a pair of binoculars is probably going too far...

But that's how you'll spot birders entering London's Tate Modern in search of one very special bird. Because the building that once housed the Bankside Power Station has been reinvented, not just as a repository for modern art, but also a space for that master of the art of hunting, the peregrine falcon.

Peregrines have been gathering on the Tate's tower since the mid noughties, part of a dramatic   bounceback for these once-common predators, which were killed deliberately during WWII to protect messenger pigeons, then driven almost to extinction by the use of the pesticide DDT in the 1950s.

Masters of the tall towers

As many as 30 breeding pairs are thought to make a home in Central London today, nesting on tall buildings such as the Tate Modern, Battersea Power Station and the Houses of Parliament. Spotting them is pure exhilaration, particularly if you are lucky enough to catch a peregrine plunging like a bullet to pluck an unsuspecting pigeon from the air.

Although small – measuring just 14in to 20in (36cm to 51cm) from head to tail – these lethal predators are grace incarnate, seeming capable of

Right: A London peregrine brings back lunch

Below: Surveying South London from the tower of Tate Modern

Q&A

How does seeing peregrine falcons make you feel?
Growing up, the peregrine was an almost mythical bird in my imagination. To encounter them in the middle of a city now is always a thrill. Knowing how close the species was to extinction, I feel privileged to be able to see such an iconic species so easily.

What makes peregrines so fast?
'Evolution' is the short answer! Peregrines have special physical adaptations which allow them to perform controlled dives at speed. Their skeletal structure and respiratory system allow them to withstand large gravitational stresses.

When's the best time to see them?
Peregrines are most active early and late in the day. At other times you might spot them perched high up on iconic structures, such as the Tate Modern, St Paul's Cathedral, Parliament or the clock tower at St Pancras station.

Stuart Harrington, London Peregrine Partnership cofounder

© Will Thomass / Shutterstock; Jeremy Selwyn / Evening Standard via Getty Images;
Wiktor Szymanowicz/Future Publishing / Getty Images; Alexey Fedorenko / Shutterstock

Left: Tate Modern and other tall buildings are perfect vantage points for peregrines

Right: Tufted ducks at the London Wetland Centre

defying gravity and executing impossible turns in midair. Seeing them at their deadly work, you really wouldn't want to be a city pigeon (or as peregrines like to call them, lunch).

Known as a 'stoop', the peregrine's dive-bomb strike can reach speeds of 200mph (322km/h). This is faster than a passenger-jet on takeoff, making these not only the fastest birds, but also the fastest animals on the planet.

An adaptable predator
In fact, pigeons only make up part of the peregrine's diet. London's invasive ring-necked parakeets are also favoured prey for peregrine falcons, alongside starlings – which moved up on the menu during the COVID-19 pandemic, when pigeons left the emptied-out city centre for suburbs still packed with crumb-dropping humans.

To spot a peregrine in London, you'll need sharp eyes and a good vantage point. The viewing decks at the Tate Modern and Battersea Power Station and the Champagne bar atop Tower 42 all do the job excellently, but you also stand a good chance at street level, looking up along the banks of the River Thames.

Once you spot a peregrine, it's worth returning to the same location for regular sightings. Tall towers such as Tate Modern have become reliable hunting and breeding grounds for falcons year after year. And if you don't spot a peregrine, you can always pop inside and see the art...

Don't Miss

→ The peregrine's graceful hover as it scans the skies for potential prey

→ Rare sightings of peregrines in their nests – if you're very lucky

→ Passing ring-necked parakeets creating flashes of colour in the cityscape

Find Your Joy

Getting there
Most of London's best peregrine-spotting sites are accessible via the Tube network. Tate Modern offers free access to its viewing deck and coffeeshop terrace. There's a fee to visit Battersea Power Station's Lift 109 viewing deck; buy a drink to access Tower 42's Vertigo 42 champagne bar.

Accessibility
London's viewing decks and riverside terraces are almost all accessible to people with limited mobility.

When to go
Peregrines are most easily spotted between July and February, with young birds making their first forays on the wing in the late summer. Scan the skies in the early morning or late afternoon for the best chance of sightings.

Further information
• Charges vary for viewing decks.
• Year-round.
• No specialist facilities but look online for webcams of peregrine nests.
• Plenty of places to stay and eat in central London; try Borough Market's stalls for a snack lunch.

© vladimir zakharov / Getty Images; kentaylordesign / Shutterstock

Other Top London Birding Sites

WWT London Wetland Centre, Barnes

A valuable wetland in the desirable London borough of Barnes, once the site of four Victorian reservoirs. Today, this calm, waterlogged space is a precious haven for visiting migrants, such as gadwalls and northern shoveler ducks, as well as kingfishers, grebes, sparrowhawks, occasional bitterns and ring-necked parakeets.

Don't miss
Staking out a spot in a hide amid the rushes to watch the bird show unfold.

Walthamstow Marshes, Walthamstow

A mixture of natural marshlands and artificial reservoirs that keep modern Londoners supplied with clean water, Walthamstow Marshes was the setting for the first British powered flight in 1909 (by Alliott Verdon Roe, of Avro aircraft company fame). Today, it's avian aviators that are the draw: look out for pochards, gadwalls, ducks, geese, swans and warblers taking off from the reservoirs.

Don't miss
The calm quiet of the marshlands, after the hectic city crush.

See ospreys & white-tailed eagles dive in Germany's lake district

 Engaging your senses, serenity, canoe trails

 White-tailed sea eagles all year, ospreys March to September

GERMANY

Day breaks and a thin mist rises above the moors, beech forests, rivers and canals that string together a necklace of ink-blue lakes in Müritz National Park. The silence is golden and the reed-fringed waters are still at this early hour. Listening intently for whistles overhead, birders suddenly catch breath as an osprey dives, talons first and rocket-fast, into the water, emerging triumphantly with a fish.

If you've never heard of this under-the-radar watery wonderland, you're not alone – but you are missing a trick. Running green and blue over 124 sq miles (322 sq km) of northeast Germany, and splashed by 130 lakes, the park delivers pristine nature and is – whisper this quietly – one of the country's birding hot-spots. Kingfishers, grey herons, bitterns, reed warblers, redshanks, black storks, cranes and little stints all appear in the avian show, but the stars are white-tailed sea eagles and ospreys.

Birding from the water
You can barely touch a map of the park without dipping your finger into a lake, and while the hiking trails are terrific, it's pure magic to birdwatch as you glide through reedy, forest-fringed waterways by canoe. With patience and good timing, the odds of raptor encounters are excellent on the 11-mile (18km) Alte Fahrt route from Mirow to the campsite at Boek, where fishponds attract hungry ospreys and white-tailed sea eagles.

Right: A white-tailed sea eagle hunting Germany's lakes

Below: More than 130 lakes are in , offering habitat to many bird species

Q&A

Why is Müritz a birding hot-spot?
The landscapes are so diverse – forest, lakes, plains, moors, each providing a safe haven for different species, from kingfishers (best spotted from a canoe) to black woodpeckers, waterfowl, birds of prey and migratory cranes.

When's the best time to see birds?
Come in spring for courtship rituals and songbirds, or summer to see ospreys and white-tailed eagles hunting on the lakes (join a guided ranger tour). In autumn, listen for the loud trumpeting of thousands of migratory cranes. Rederang Lake is a fine spot for witnessing this incredible spectacle.

Where's a good spot to watch?
Head to the Boek fishponds to see ospreys and white-tailed eagles at close range. The Federow visitor centre has a webcam looking directly into an osprey's nest. Make sure you bring binoculars!

Eike Lucas, Müritz National Park head of environmental education

© Maralee Park / Shutterstock; Ina Meer Sommer / Shutterstock;
Jerry Bouwmeester / Shutterstock; Image Professionals GmbH / Alamy Stock Photo

En route, look out for the electric-blue flash of kingfishers on the water-lily-spattered Kotzowsee.

For a longer tour, the two-day, 24-mile (39km) Obere Havel route from Kratzenberg to Zwenzow is a twitcher's dream, with the Havel River threading from lake to glorious lake, past woodland and marshy meadows.

Osprey & eagle alert

There's nothing quite like glimpsing an osprey on the hunt. Returning from Africa in spring, these magnificent raptors can be spotted in Müritz until early October. Identify them by their shrill chirps and whistles, kinked wings (from below they resemble a perfect 'M'), hooked beak and distinctive mottled plumage. Federow on the shores of Hofsee is a great place to spot them hunting, as an eyrie tops a pylon close by, which means you can observe them from a respectful distance and – if all else fails – see them up close on the visitor

centre webcam.

With their 6.5ft (2m) wingspan, white-tailed eagles are equally impressive, screeching and soaring like glider planes before diving from a height of 190ft (60m), plummeting down and plucking a flapping fish from the lake with their talons. The park is home to some 300 pairs of white-tailed eagles, with sightings most common in summer. The Boek ponds are one of their favourite hangouts for a fish feast, or grab binoculars and head up to one of the park's lake-facing observation platforms.

Right: Cranes in formation over Rederangsee in Müritz National Park

Far right: Different ducks bobbing on Lake Constance

Don't Miss

→ **Glimpsing an osprey dive deep to catch its prey**

→ **Seeing mighty white-tailed eagles in flight**

→ **Spotting kingfishers dart from the reeds as you paddle the lakes**

Find Your Joy

Getting there

Midway between Berlin and Rostock in northeast Germany, Müritz feels remote, but the main

gateway, Waren at the northern tip of Lake Müritz, is a 1¼-hour train ride from Berlin. Regional trains run hourly from Berlin to Mirow (journey time is two hours). Once there, explore on foot, by bike or canoe: all towns have rental facilities.

Accessibility

The Federow and Boek visitor centre have

wheelchair-accessible access; observation platforms at Hofsee near Federow and the Boek fishponds are also wheelchair-accessible.

When to go

Ospreys return to the park from their African wintering grounds around late March and stay until spring. Other birdlife, including white-tailed sea

eagles, grey herons and kingfishers, can be spotted year-round.

Further information

- Free to visitors.
- Open year-round.
- Wildlife lookouts and ranger tours.
- Cafes and restaurants.
- Camping and holiday rentals in the park.
- www.mueritz-nationalpark.de

© Imago Professionals GmbH / Alamy Stock Photo; Thomas Schnarr / Imago Stock Photo

Other Birding Hot-spots in Germany

Hiddensee

This Baltic island at Germany's northern cusp is a birding delight, with frost-white sands, forest, heathland and salt marshes battered by wind and wave. Rügen's smaller, slender, quieter neighbour, Hiddensee is a migratory stop-off for waders, ducks and geese in winter and spring. Species of note include demoiselle cranes, little stints, broad-billed sandpipers and Eurasian oystercatchers.

Don't miss

The autumn massed migration of cranes, best observed in Hiddensee's lighthouse-topped north.

Lake Constance

Where three countries (Germany, Austria and Switzerland) converge and the Alps pucker up on the horizon, Lake Constance acts as a year-round magnet to birds. Spring, autumn and winter are prime time for twitching, with magic spots including the Wollmatinger marshes near Konstanz. Keep an eye out for waterfowl like black-necked grebes, grey herons, gadwalls, teals, water pipits and goosanders.

Don't miss

The spring honk of whooper swans and nightingale concerts in April and May at the lake's northern Eriskirch marshes.

See the synchronised swooping of Cornish choughs

 Reintroduced species, Celtic mythology, historic buildings

 September to March

UK

You could be forgiven for thinking you'd stumbled upon a litter of stray cats if you wander around the Cornish coast. Among the ruins of what was once Cornwall's most important industry – a tin, copper and arsenic mining trade that lasted almost 300 years – you'll hear the mews of an endemic species that was once declared extinct in this region. Mingling with the whoosh of wind and the crashing of waves on rocks, the call of the Cornish chough has found its home here once again.

A small, energetic bird with black feathers and a red beak and legs, this Cornish character disappeared from the region in the 1970s, after a steady decline in numbers over more than a

hundred years. In 2001, a surprise sighting on the Lizard Peninsula – the most southerly mainland point in the British Isles – heralded the Cornish chough's return.

Rather ironically for such a patriotically named bird, these newcomers actually arrived from Ireland. But 20 years later, thanks to the conservation efforts of the RSPB, there are more than 200 resident choughs in Cornwall.

Choughs on the mining trails

Today, you'll spy them on the Cornish section of the South West Coast Path, which runs for some 330 miles (531km) through a landscape littered with the remnants of the mining industry. Derelict stone chimneys and crumbling engine houses cling resolutely to cliffs almost as black as

Right: The Crowns engine houses in the Botallack mining area at the tip of Cornwall

Below: Cornish choughs have big personalities

Q&A

Why did Cornish choughs disappear?
Although engine houses now provide an ideal nesting ground for choughs, the mining industry contributed to their habitat destruction, as did farming. They were also targets for trophy hunters and egg collectors.

Where can I spot them here?
Near Land's End, from Penberth around to St Ives.

Where else can you find them?
Largely in coastal areas of Brittany, Wales, Northern Spain, Scotland, Northern Ireland, the Isle of Man and the Canary Islands. They're also found in the Himalayas (where the bird is known as the red-billed chough).

Why are they so important here?
They're on the Cornish emblem, along with a fisherman and a tin miner. They're a symbol of national pride!

Nicola Shanks, RSPB volunteer specialising in Cornish choughs

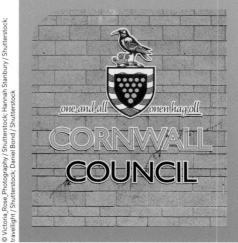

one and all · onen hag oll

CORNWALL COUNCIL

© Victoria_Rose_Photography / Shutterstock; Hannah Stanbury / Shutterstock; travelight / Shutterstock; Daniel Bond / Shutterstock

Left: Kynance Cove on Cornwall's Lizard Peninsula

Right: Peninnis Lighthouse on St Mary's in the Isles of Scilly

into a nearby crow, turning its legs and long bill a bloody red and transforming the crow into the Cornish chough that we know today.

Chatty, dancing birds

Whether their legs are filled with the blood of an ancient king or not, choughs are a sight to behold. Pairs swoop in formation, one diving down as its partner flies up, moving like synchronised dancers – a motion that brings to mind the ebb and flow of waves on Cornish beaches. Chatty, sociable birds, their cat-mew call is easy to identify.

They also have a trust of humans, something that contributed to their extinction, as they were easy prey for trophy hunters. For modern photographers, good shots are easy to come by, particularly when the choughs are framed against a backdrop of scarred engine houses and a tempestuous sea.

Don't Miss

→ **A windswept stomp along the old mining trails**

→ **Watching choughs duck and dive over the waves**

→ **Catching congregations of choughs at sunset**

the chough's plumage, and green copper ore pools in iridescent patterns down the rocks.

When not nesting in mineshafts, choughs seek out crevasses in cliff faces, so the coastal path is one of the best places to see them. The choughs chack noisily and dive in the wind, like moving smudges of black; you'll have to look closely to spot their red beak and legs.

They've been the source of many local legends, including the myth that when King Arthur was fatally wounded at the Battle of Camlann, his blood poured

Find Your Joy

5½ hours. Cornwall Birdwatching Tours (www. cornwall-birding.co.uk) operates tours from Hayle (pickups elsewhere can often be arranged). Tours typically last a full day (take a packed lunch) and cost from £80.

Getting there
Direct trains run between London and Penzance, in the heart of chough country, taking roughly

Accessibility
The Cornish coastal path is difficult for those with mobility issues, as it tends to be uneven, steep, and often incredibly muddy. The best bet is to book onto an organised tour and ask about your needs in advance if you're unsure.

When to go
Choughs can be spotted year-round, but tread lightly to avoid disturbing them during the nesting season (March to May). To see them in larger groups,

visit from September to February, when the chicks have hatched.

Further information
• Free access to the Coast Path.
• Open year-round.
• No designated bird hides.
• Stay at Artist Residence, Penzance (artistresidence.co.uk)

© Skowronek / Shutterstock; Kath Watson / Shutterstock

Other Cornish Birding Sites

Isles of Scilly

Around 28 miles (45km) from the Cornish coast, the Isles of Scilly look like a tropical archipelago, with shimmering beaches and plants endemic to much sunnier climes. But birders are drawn by the 17 species of seabird that breed here, including puffins, storm petrels and Manx shearwaters.

Don't miss

Looking for stripe-faced little whinchats from Peninnis Lighthouse during the summer, when the birds migrate up from Africa.

Botallack Engine Houses, Penzance

From the same family as Cornish choughs, jet-black jackdaws are also easy to spot nesting in abandoned engine houses. Visit the Botallack Engine Houses, where a steep cliff path goes all the way down to the old buildings, winding through purple knapweed and hogweed, and look for nests built of twigs and bracken in the old chimneys.

Don't miss

Looking jackdaws in the eye – their irises are a creamy white, in startling contrast to their black plumage.

Witness magical murmurations in the Eternal City

 Wonder, effortless choreography, spontaneous encounters

 November to February

ITALY

Legend has it that before major battles, ancient Roman mystics would look to the heavens for a sign. But they weren't looking at the planets – they were casting their eyes toward the breathtaking movement of starlings, which could darken the skies in an instant, simply by banding together in vast, swirling murmurations.

Today, the starlings still return to Rome each November, filling the evening skies in undulating, otherworldly masses until they move on to Northern Europe in February. But even naturalists can't fully explain how hundreds of thousands of birds can move so tightly, in such perfect choreography. How do they find each other, or find their way back here? Somewhere in between birdwatching and stargazing, there is the sight of a flight of starlings, cascading over the rooftops of Rome.

Nightly gossip
Though starling murmurations have long been a subject of fascination, they've become increasingly common in Rome, particularly since starlings began nesting in and around the city in the 1970s.

Though we don't know quite how they murmurate, we do have some idea of why. Like the sardine, this diminutive bird finds strength in numbers; the more they gather and the more spellbinding their dance, the more chance they have of surviving predators.

Moreover, the starling is a social animal whose daily routine consists of morning excursions to feed on the olive trees that grow prolifically around Rome before returning to the city for

Right: The structure of starlings' feathers creates their colours

Below: A murmuration of starlings over the church of Santissima Trinità dei Monti in Rome

Q&A

Is birdwatching popular in Italy? Is that why you decided to create tours?
It is increasingly widespread, but people don't realise just how many species of birds there are in Italy. My partners Valerio and Luca (who are also both wildlife professionals) and I developed the idea of birding day trips departing from Rome and other cities like Naples to show that there is so much to see right in front of us.

Where's the best place to see starlings in Rome?
A very popular observation site is Piazza dei Cinquecento near Termini Station, but the birds also form roosts in other places around the city. This is great for nature enthusiasts but less so for drivers, given the amount of guano they produce!

Where would you send people to see them?
The Janiculum, Tiber Island or the Verano Cemetery.

Andrea Senese, K' Nature cofounder

© amer ghazzal / Alamy Stock Photo; arjma / Shutterstock; Stefano Tammaro / Shutterstock

their crepuscular gatherings. Perhaps the murmuration is their way of catching up on the news of the day, with massed avian reporters updating the flock on the various corners of their world. Maybe this is a social dance – as much about movement as conversation – and we have the privilege of being able to watch it all unfold.

Right: Enjoy an aperitivo at sunset and you might get a show of starlings

Far right: The Temple of Aesculapius in in the gardens of the Villa Borghese

A true Roman holiday

Any party worth talking about is also going to need cleaning up, and the starling murmuration is no exception. The guano left in their wake throughout the city is perhaps as legendary as the spectacle of their murmurations; the Roman authorities have tried – and mostly failed – to discourage this particular form of mass tourism, so don't forget your (protective) umbrella. Regrettably, climate change may prove a more effective deterrent. Increasing global temperatures are disrupting

everything from migratory patterns to breeding seasons and nesting areas for many bird species, and, sadly, the starling is no exception.

Like all things worth protecting, Rome's starling murmurations are ephemeral and delicate. If you find yourself here, walking on the cobblestones as the January sun starts to set, look to the skies for some divine inspiration. You might just find that it is not the stars that shine back at you but the swooping backs of a million silvery surfers.

Don't Miss

→ **Murmuration views from the Janiculum**

→ **Aperitivo at sunset in the ancient centre**

→ **Front-row starling-watching seats at alfresco cafes**

Find Your Joy

Getting there
The Piazza dei Cinquecento is in the centre of Rome, just outside of Termini Station.

Both the A and B metro lines stop there, along with bus lines. To view starlings from the Janiculum, use bus lines 75 and 115 from Termini. Verano Cemetery is connected to Termini via the 14 tram or bus line 71; the Tiber Island is best reached on foot. Note that it can be messy beneath the starlings: bring an umbrella or a poncho.

Accessibility
Because the starling murmurations move over the city, it's easy to find an accessible viewpoint. There is a slope to cross onto the Tiber Island, but the Verano Cemetery has accessible shuttles that transport visitors around the grounds.

When to Go
Starlings typically arrive in Rome in November and remain until February, they return to Northern Europe as the weather gets warmer.

Further Information
• Free to visitors.
• No specialist facilities.
• Close to the Vatican, Mama Shelter has a rooftop bar plus rooms.
• www.turismoroma.it

© Tim F White / Getty Images; Kiev Victor / Shutterstock

Other Lazio Birding Locations

Villa Borghese

The bucolic but central Villa Borghese park is a prime birding spot and one of the city's nicest places for respite in nature after (or during) a hectic day. Visit the priceless collections of the magnificent Galleria Borghese, then wander the grounds and keep an eye out for yellow-legged gulls, wagtails, robins and both great and blue tits.

Don't miss

The rose-ringed and monk parakeets that have made Rome their unlikely home.

Parco Nazionale del Circeo

About 50 miles (80km) south of Rome, and encompassing wetlands, sand dunes and four coastal lakes, Circeo is one of the oldest protected areas in Italy and hosts hundreds of species of nesting, wintering and migrating birds. Hike the well-marked trails up to Mt Circeo, 1775ft (541m) above sea level, and share the views with herons and cormorants.

Don't miss

The tender migratory dance of flamingos on Lake Caprolace.

Scan coastal waters off the Ninase Peninsula in search of Steller's eider

 Towering seas, exquisite plumage, rare sightings

 March to mid-April

ESTONIA

On the coast of Saaremaa's Ninase Peninsula, rolling surf crashes on to the shingle shoreline, the horizon difficult to discern against a leaden, grey-on-grey sky. The continual, repetitive movement of the waves creates an almost hypnotic calm – but suddenly, a colourful jewel appears riding a crest, offering a split second of ecstasy for the onlooking birdwatchers before it's swallowed up again by the sea.

Did it really happen? Yes! The image of the drake Steller's eider is firmly burnt on to their retinas. With all telescopes now trained on the area, the bird appears again atop the next advancing wave, allowing more time to savour this rare species in all its glory. The orange sides, shading to chestnut on its breast, distinguish it from the flocks of nearby long-tailed ducks, and as the birders get their eye in, the sea reveals more Steller's eiders, first scattered and then in a small flock, the inconspicuous brown females easy to overlook were they not consorting with the gaudily plumaged males.

In the distance flocks of common scoter, occasionally joined by rarer velvet scoters, pass by offshore, flying low over the waves as they head north on their migration. Soon the eiders will join them on this journey.

Small ducks on the high seas

The Steller's eider breeds in the high Arctic and spends

Right: The distinctive plumage of the Steller's eider duck

Below: Male and female Steller's eider ducks flying off Saaremaa Island

Q&A

Why is the Steller's eider such a special bird in Estonia?
It's one of Europe's most endangered and most beautiful sea ducks. Saaremaa Island is probably the most easily accessible place to see them in Europe.

Any other species to look out for while here?
I would look for parrot crossbills, pygmy owls, common and velvet scoters, snow buntings, smew, white-tailed eagles, nutcrackers, waxwings and, during some years, the northern hawk-owl.

What does Saaremaa Island mean to you?
For me, it's usually the place where the spring arrives first in Estonia. So going there means the beginning of the touring season, and I get to experience the arrival of spring firsthand.

What are your other favourite birding destinations in Estonia?
Probably the western coast (Matsalu National Park and the northwestern area), also Lahemaa National Park for forest birds.

Peep Rooks, Estonian bird guide

© Sergey Uryadnikov / Shutterstock; KEVIN ELSBY / Alamy Stock Photo;

Left: A traditional windmill on the northern Ninase Peninsula of Saaremaa Island

Right: Exploring reed-filled waterways of Matsalu National Park

much of the winter out at sea. It's the smallest and rarest of the various eider species and the most distantly related, possibly providing a 'missing link' between eiders and other sea ducks. The male's white head contrasts with its black cap and neck collar, with splodges of green in front of the eye and on the back of the head adding a finishing touch. The black-and-white wings and black rear-end set off the orangey underside, with its prominent black spot.

As is often the case in the bird world, the female is a rather dowdier affair, being mainly brown – though this is useful camouflage when sitting on a nest in the marshy Arctic tundra. These tundra ponds are disappearing due to climate change, however, creating the greatest threat to the survival of the species.

The bay and beyond

Back in the bay, on more sheltered waters, a red-necked grebe, still in winter plumage and therefore failing to live up to its name, consorts with commoner relatives like the great crested grebe. A single male smew sails by, its pale plumage and crest giving it its colloquial name of 'white nun'. As the afternoon sun fades, pandemonium breaks out amongst the gaggles of geese feeding in the fields along the water's edge, as a passing white-tailed eagle seeks its final meal of the day. It sails on beyond the tip of the peninsula, and calm is restored.

Don't Miss

→ Scanning the breaking waves for Steller's eiders

→ Listening out for bugling pairs of common cranes

→ Sampling the local speciality drink, silky and slightly sweet birch-tree sap

Find Your Joy

hop to Kuivastu on Muhu Island. It's then a 1½-hour drive across Muhu and the causeway to Saaremaa to reach Loona, 19 miles (30km) southwest of the Ninase Peninsula and a good base. NaTourEst (www.natourest.ee) offer eider-spotting tours and self-guided options (an app provides pins for birding locations, towers, trails and possible species).

Accessibility
You can see Steller's eiders from your vehicle at Saaremaa Sadam's harbour car park, overlooking Küdema Laht bay. Accessing the Ninase Peninsula's northern shore means a short walk over shingle.

When to go
Flocks of Steller's eider gather closer to shore between March and mid-April, after the sea ice has melted and before they migrate to their Arctic breeding grounds.

Further information
• Free access all year
• No specialist facilities.
• Rooms and a restaurant at Loona Manor Guesthouse.
• www.visitsaaremaa.ee

Getting there
From Virtsu's port, 1¾ hours' drive southwest of Tallinn, car and passenger ferries (www.praamid.ee)

© robertharding / Alamy Stock Photo; F-Focus by Mati Kose / Shutterstock

Other Estonian Birding Sites

Nõva Nature Reserve

On the mainland to the northeast of Saaremaa, and with a visitor centre at Peraküla, Nõva Nature Reserve is defined by sand dunes, bogs and pine forests, and is home to some very special bird species. Walk the forest trails to seek out sightings of the diminutive hazel grouse – inquisitive enough to investigate the call from a hunter's whistle.

Don't miss
Spotting the turkey-sized male capercaillie strutting across the forest floor.

Matsalu National Park

Encompassing Northern Europe's largest flood meadow (an increasingly rare habitat), Matsalu National Park offers an ideal habitat for woodpeckers, with sightings of black, white-backed, middle-spotted and grey-headed varieties all likely throughout the park. There's a visitor centre at Penijõe Manor, just off the Tallinn–Virtsu road, and bird observation towers a at Haeska, Kloostri and Keemu.

Don't miss
Searching for three-toed woodpeckers in Palivere Forest to the north.

Spot barn owls on the hunt in a Dordogne château

 Unique hunting tactics, history, medieval architecture

 Early November & December

FRANCE

At a lofty castle in the Dordogne, a flash of white appears in the night sky. It flits past the 13th-century turrets, its plumage brilliantly illuminated in the moonlight. Some might claim they've seen something supernatural – but this splendid spectre is a barn owl on the hunt.

The barn owl is the only nocturnal avian hunter with bright-white plumage, and it uses this to its advantage. Rather than passing incognito, camouflaged, it exploits the white underside of its wings to startle the small rodents that it hunts, triggering a 'rabbit in the headlights' reaction. It hunts best under the full moon, when the moonlight reflects on its feathers.

Haunting or hunting?
Barn owls nesting in the eaves of châteaux have been the source of supernatural 'sightings' all across France. In the southwest Dordogne, the Château de Puymartin is reputed to be among the country's most haunted sites – thanks to the spectral presence of one Thérèse de Saint-Clar, who died here in grisly circumstances during the 16th century.

Reported sightings of her 'white lady' ghost around the North Tower are frequent, but this part of the building is also the home of nesting barn owls. An exhibition inside the château delves into the numerous occasions when barn owls have been mistaken for ghosts here.

190 Europe

Right: Barns are preferred accommodation for barn owls

Below: The Château de Puymartin, home of barn owls and not ghosts

What's special about barn owls?
Barn owls don't fight, they negotiate. When parents return from hunting with a mouse, they often have up to eight young in a nest. Instead of sharing the mouse out like a cake, the young prioritise who is hungriest, and that chick receives the mouse.

How did you discover that barn owls use the fear factor to hunt?
We made a zip line with models of barn owls and sent them whizzing down a wire over caged voles to analyse their responses.

Why is their spooky vibe an issue?
Their association with bad luck and superstition. Recently a man in Nigeria killed and burnt a barn owl because he believed it had an evil witch's spirit inside. They're maligned in many different countries!

Alexandre Roulin, academic and author of Barn Owls: Evolution and Ecology

© New Africa / Shutterstock; Pack-Shot / Shutterstock; Helen J Davies / Shutterstock; PJR-Photography / Shutterstock

Wait until the sun sets

As dusk falls at Puymartin, most visitors depart this lonely spot. On a clear night, the stars and moonlight illuminate the *Rapunzel*-like towers, towering high above the surrounding woodland. To be in with a good chance of spotting barn owls (or indeed the elusive 'white lady'), you'll need to visit Puymartin when the nights draw in, from early November to around Christmas.

Look up at the turret of the North Tower from the gardens to see barn owls hunting silently. When they do make a noise, it's bloodcurdling. Unlike the soft hooting of most owl species, barn owls emit a long, harsh screech that lasts several seconds.

A harbinger of misfortune?

Despite the loss of many of the old buildings in which they nest, barn owls are thriving. They're found in abundance on all continents except Antarctica, and the world population is estimated

Right: Soft feathers help barn owls fly silently

Far right: The Château de Castelnau-Bretenoux in the Lot region

at between four and 10 million. Nonetheless, barn owls have long been associated with bad luck, wherever they live.

Roman superstition had it that the spirits of witches turned into barn owls, and among Native American cultures, barn owls are said to be the reincarnation of weak warriors. But if you do see one of these beautiful birds, you may well feel lucky indeed. With a wingspan of up to 4ft (1.2m), there's an elegance to the way they fly – and seen up close, their heart-shaped faces look cuddly rather than creepy.

Don't Miss

→ **Watching owls swoop on startled voles under the full moon**

→ **Feeling goosebumps hearing ghost stories during your visit to the château**

→ **The castle exhibits on the links between the 'white lady' and barn owls**

Find Your Joy

Getting there
The closest train station is in St-Cyprien, two hours by rail from Bordeaux (which has

an international airport and high-speed train connections with Paris). From here, Puymartin is a 15-minute (8-mile/13km) drive.

Accessibility
There's free parking on-site, but neither the château nor the gardens are accessible to those in wheelchairs or with impaired mobility.

When to go
To spot barn owls at the Château de Puymartin, visit late in the day when there's less light. In early November or December the last entry is at 4.30pm, and the castle and grounds stay open until 5.30pm.

Further information
• Admission fee.
• Château de Puymartin is

open from 1 April to 11 November, and during the Christmas holidays.
• No specialist facilities.
• Accommodation and eating options in Sarlat-la-Canéda, 5 miles (8km) from Puymartin.
• www.chateau-puymartin.com

Other Châteaux for Birders

Château de Castelnau-Bretenoux, Lot

Holes in the 11th-century walls here provide perfect ready-made nests for local birdlife, and the castle is equipped with nesting boxes, too. Book onto one of the guided visits in conjunction with the Ligue pour la Protection des Oiseaux (Birds' Protection League), some of which run at night to spot owls and bats.

Don't miss

The panoramic view (and bird sightings) from the top of the artillery tower.

Château d'Amboise, Indre-et-Loire

Some 82 bird species nest in the castle ramparts and gardens, and 22 nesting boxes have been installed here to encourage this. Chickadees, kestrels, swallows and swifts are among the birds that make their homes here, but there are several owl species too, notably a tawny owl that lives in the large cedar tree in the grounds.

Don't miss

Spotting wallcreepers, sometimes seen perched by gargoyles.

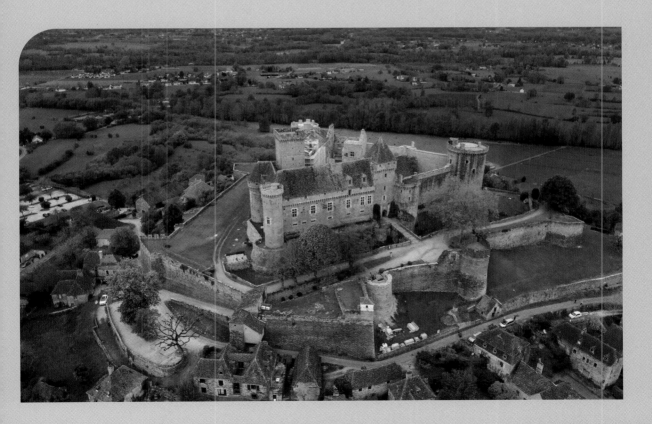

Peer up pylons & poles to see nesting white storks

♡ Extraordinary sounds, awesome nests, close encounters

🕐 March to July is nesting season

PORTUGAL

Hear that? Listen, closely, to the sound of rapid pulsations. Could it be the rhythmic beat of distant castanets? Quiet and then louder, it ebbs and flows like controlled drumbeats, sometimes barely loud enough to be distinguished from the ambient noise. Discovering the source – like an aural, not visual, game of I-spy – is both astonishing and exhilarating.

So where is it coming from? Peer upwards. There's a bird standing atop its nest – a colossal, messy conglomeration of sticks poised atop a telephone pole. There's another, above an electricity pylon. And yet another above a chimney! In fact, a long line of poles – all topped with nests – extends along the block, creating a feather-focused residential neighbourhood.

Welcome to the awe-inspiring 'stork country' of Portugal's Alentejo region.

Protected under Portuguese law, white storks and their nests have become an integral part of Portuguese villages and the rural landscape, especially in and around Alentejo villages such as Castro Verde, Mértola and Odiáxere. It's mind-boggling viewing these graceful birds that, with their red beaks, long legs and white-and-black plumage, resemble lanky athletes in team uniform.

Residents of the rooftops

Witnessing these remarkable birds is one thing; understanding their behaviour enhances the experience. Storks (in general) mate for life, reuniting each nesting season, though more and more storks are becoming residents as they

Right: Storks in Alentejo don't mind nesting in proximity to people

Below: Storks foraging for food with the help of a farmer

Q&A

Why are storks so special?
They're so flexible and adaptable to environmental change. They manage to live in human-dominated landscapes, even within urban spaces. And they even changed their migratory practices recently! (Most storks used to be migratory. In 1994, the resident population of storks in Portugal was 18%; by 2014 this had increased to 62%.)

If you were a stork, where would you nest, and why?
I'd nest in a high tower that's on the edge of Faro (Algarve) for the wide views of the estuary and salt marshes.

And, a resident or a migratory stork?
Definitely migratory. I would want to see Africa! Although it's a lot more risky and the mortality is higher for migratory birds; around 65% do not survive beyond the first year of life. We think it's associated with their migration and stay in Africa (where they're hunted), along with the weather, especially crossing the Sahara (due to sandstorms).

Aldina Franco, stork specialist and academic

© Emily Marie Wilson / Shutterstock; MariaSousa / Shutterstock; tilialucida / Shutterstock

Left: Sometimes humans in the Alentejo lend a hand with nest-building

Right: Rühstädt in Germany is a Unesco Biosphere Reserve

Living the high life

The hypnotic vision of watching storks soaring – riding a thermal, their massive wings spread over a 6.5ft (2m) span – is a high of a different kind. Few sights evoke such a meditative sense of calm. And watching them when they're on the ground is equally as amazing: such as when, having congregated in a field, they walk forwards in a line to catch grasshoppers, resembling an earnest police-search party looking for evidence.

But there's no greater wonder than to see a stork returning to its nest, upon which the waiting mate claps its beak in castanet style. So do the chicks – whose fluffy feathers you might be lucky to glimpse, especially as they grow to fledglings – as they eagerly greet a returning parent.

The fact that, year after year, this occurs within our visible orbit, often a mere pole-length away, is a rare privilege indeed.

Don't Miss

→ **Driving between the villages to watch flocks of storks riding the thermals**

→ **Viewing a nest at eye level in Mértola**

→ **The surprising sound of beak-clapping**

adapt to environment changes. If a stork loses a partner because it has migrated and its return timing is not perfect, they'll take up with another.

During mating season, it's fascinating to see a duo repairing and building up their nest: they shake each stick into place, sometimes increasing the weight of their nests to an astonishing 1 ton or thereabouts. After the female lays her three to five eggs, you can observe the storks switching between the roles of incubator and hunter, as they hunt (or scavenge) for food.

Find Your Joy

Getting there
The Alentejo is south of Lisbon and Estremadura, and north of the Algarve. The most accessible city,

Évora, is 2½ hours from Lisbon by car or bus.

Accessibility
The beauty of spotting storks is that you can do so from a vehicle. Some villages are accessible for wheelchair users but others, such as Mértola, have limited access due to their medieval-style pedestrian alleyways.

When to go
You can see storks all year round. Due to climate change (and the abundance of food available throughout the year), the storks are starting to breed as early as February/beginning of March to end of July. In May you can see fledglings leaving their nests.

Further information
• Free to visitors.
• Year-round.
• No specialist facilities.
• Accommodation and places to eat and drink in and around Mértola and other Alentejo villages.
• www.storkvillages.net highlights European villages with stork colonies.

© trattieritratti / Shutterstock; dpa picture alliance / Alamy Stock Photo

Other White Stork Locations

Żywkowo, Poland

Between April and August, around 25% of the total global population of white storks migrates to Poland. Many Poles believe that stork nests bring luck and protection against fires and lightning strikes. It's claimed that there are four times as many storks as people in the village of Żywkowo, in northeast Poland, where single houses often have several nests atop the roof.

Don't miss
Visiting Żywkowo's Polish Society for the Protection of Birds field station, with a watchtower for birdwatching and excellent local information.

Rühstädt, Germany

Located at the confluence of the Elbe and Havel Rivers, the village of Rühstädt in Brandenburg is famous for its resident white storks; around 30 or so breeding pairs return annually to raise their young atop rooftops in the village.

Don't miss
Heading out to see storks en masse as they feed in the floodplains around Rühstädt.

Family fun with hoopoes in the Sierra de Bernia

♡ Mountain scenery, family birding, wildlife visitors

🕐 April to early June & October

SPAIN

'Look! There they are! There!' Casually trotting across the garden of our rented mountain finca (country cottage), a pair of zebra-striped, punk-hairdo-sporting hoopoes is all it takes to distract the children from a competitive Uno marathon.

Our stillness as we sit playing cards has made the birds bolder. We watch as they parade stylishly before swiftly exiting stage right behind a spiky yucca. As we're used to the familiarity of garden birds back in the UK, the hoopoes, with their curving beaks and artistic sweep of head feathers, feel impossibly glamorous.

A biodiverse buffet for birds
Inland from the Costa Blanca, the undeveloped expanse of the Sierra de Bernia offers

peace and space, but also – crucially for a family looking for wildlife – impressive biodiversity, supporting many endemic and migrating birds.

We're based at the end of a winding mountain road that turns into a track before swinging into the green-and-brown bowl of a valley sculpted by olive terraces. The wooded slopes surrounding old stone farms in Refugio Marnes are covered by preservation orders, protecting vital habitats for birds. Rocks and pine needles harbour spiders, almonds ripen and fall to the ground, and figs burst on the bough, attracting lines of ants, drones of wasps and heavy, hovering beetles – sustenance for an ever-changing avian roster.

Lazy mountain days
Our friends, the hoopoes, have

Right: Hoopoes have extremely strong beaks for foraging and fighting

Below: When incubating eggs, female hoopoes smear them in an antibacterial concoction

Q&A

There's more to eastern Spain than the beaches, right?
When I first started coming to the Valencia region 20 years ago, I was really surprised by the diversity of habitats. There are the mountains, but also rich wetlands all along the coast.

What are the top spots for birding?
Birds when they migrate follow flyways – there's one that follows the east coast of Spain. The birds will use the system of wetlands to rest and feed. For families with younger children, wetlands are great because aquatic birds tend to be still for longer.

Best time to catch this migration?
October. The autumn migration is much slower than the spring when the birds are biologically under pressure to get to a nesting site.

Favourite bird?
The swift. They are the sound of my childhood summers in Yorkshire.

David Warrington, Valencia Birding founder (valenciabirding.com)

© Bildagentur Zoonar GmbH / Shutterstock/ Karel Stipek / Shutterstock

© Miguel AF / Shutterstock Maionit / Shutterstock

long, pointed beaks – perfectly adapted to sifting through leaves and stones for bugs. With the summer heat, they tend to make brisk and exciting appearances at dawn and dusk – perfect timing for the kids' inbuilt alarm clocks. Other birds appear too, and we marvel at the arrow of a swift diving for flies, or an eagle hovering above the treeline. As the light fades, the wildlife changes. Sleek and secretive pine martens dart between distant trees, and bats play in the sky above our heads.

We fall into a routine of eating breakfast in the shade of fig trees, chasing the moving shadows as the heat rises. In the quiet of the valley, we hear the lyrical call and response of a pair of late-season nightingales, the tinkly chorus of a charm of goldfinches, the distinctive 'hoop-hoop-hoop' of hoopoes.

Shy Spanish residents

Hoopoes can be found year-round in southern Spain but are notoriously shy. We only catch the occasional flashes of black-and-white feathers after our first hoopoe parade, but what else would you expect from the rock star of the avian world? You have to keep the crowd waiting…

There are many more birds to spot, however. A bird-ID app is worth its weight in data: it is pure magic to hold your phone up to the sky and watch together as it identifies warblers, flycatchers and, yes, the occasional hoopoe.

Right: The mountainous landscape of the Sierra de Bernia

Far right: Get around by boat in Valencia's Albufera nature reserve

Don't Miss

→ Hearing tawny owls call to each other in the dark

→ The dawn chorus before the heat rises

→ Scraping the tastiest crusts of rice from a paella pan

Find Your Joy

Getting there

By car, the Sierra de Bernia is an hour from Alicante airport and about 1¾ hours from Valencia airport. From Alicante, drive past Altea, taking a left turn at Benissa onto the winding mountain road to Refugio Marnes (www.refugiomarnes.com).

Accessibility

While Sierra de Bernia lacks infrastructure for wheelchair users and those with mobility issues, nearby regional wetlands, including the Parque Natural de la Marjal de Pego Oliva, have accessible walkways.

When to go

The spring breeding season (April to early June) sees lots of bird movement; in October and November, birds make their (slower) migration back to Africa. During July and August, birds tend to hide during the heat of the day.

Further information
• Year-round.
• No fees to access the mountains.
• No specialist facilities.
• There are a handful of restaurants a 10-minute drive away.
• Refugio Marnes has glamping and finca accommodation.
• www. comunitatvalenciana. com

Other Valencia Birding Hot-spots

Parque Natural de la Albufera

Some 6 miles (10km) south of Valencia city, Parque Natural de la Albufera is the region's best-known wetland area. It's a huge dune and freshwater ecosystem, most of which is ricefields – the area is the birthplace of paella. Around 90 bird species regularly nest here, and up to 300 others use it as a migratory staging post.

Don't miss

Sighting colourful flamingos, a hit with any young bird enthusiast.

Parque Natural de la Marjal de Pego Oliva

Between Alicante and Valencia cities, and beautifully framed by a horseshoe of mountains, the Pego Oliva marshes contain underwater springs, making this an important nesting and feeding habitat. The site is at the centre of a project to reintroduce ospreys to the region, but many bird species can be seen while walking or cycling around the marsh and adjoining ricefields.

Don't miss

Settling in with binoculars as herons and egrets go about their watery lives.

Watch griffon vultures soar & scavenge in the French Pyrenees

 Magnificent flyers, rare bearded vultures, passing migrants

 April to May, & September to October

FRANCE

The landscape is cold and grey, with fingers of mist feeling their way through the bare branches of winter trees. All is silent, but then, quite suddenly, a bloodcurdling screech, which sounds as if it was emitted by the Grim Reaper himself, echoes back and forth across the hills. Meet the griffon vulture – one of Europe's largest and most enigmatic birds.

The vast beech forests of Iraty (Irati in Spanish) are an idyll on a warm sunny day when the soft, mossy banks of the streams that lace through the hills are filled with picnicking families. But given the region's position at the Atlantic Ocean end of the Pyrenees, the hills and forests here are often obscured under thick, low cloud. And when that happens, Iraty takes on a darker and more sinister tone...

The devil's own bird

If you climb higher, you'll find the source of that terrifying screech. As you gain altitude, the mists of the valley forests start to dissipate and beams of wispy sunlight scuttle over the grassy summits. And there they are – a pack of them, bickering loudly with one another over whose turn it is to tear a morsel of flesh off the carcass of an unfortunate sheep that fell off a cliff face. If the devil had a pet bird, then it would have to be a griffon vulture.

Right: A bare head and neck helps griffon vultures stay cool and clean

Below: Griffon vultures gliding on thermals in the Pyrenees

© Rudmer Zwerver / Shutterstock; fsanz / Shutterstock; Rudmer Zwerver / Shutterstock; Bouke Atema / Shutterstock

Q&A

Every time you look up in the Pyrenees, it seems there's a vulture circling. How many are there?
In the whole of the Pyrenees there are 200 pairs of bearded vultures and the population is growing by 3.5% per year. Regarding the populations of griffon and Egyptian vultures, I only know the populations for the province of Huesca (Aragon, Spain), but in this area there are 1700 pairs of griffon vultures and 140 pairs of Egyptian vultures.

Iraty is a superb place to see vultures, but can you tell us your favourite spots?
For me, the best place in the world to observe bearded vultures is the Gorges d'Escuaín in Spain's Parque Nacional de Ordesa y Monte Perdido. You can also see lots of griffon and Egyptian vultures here.

Juan Antonio Gil, founding member of the Fundación para la Conservación del Quebrantahuesos (FCQ).

Left: The Pyrenees are a beautiful destination for hiking

Right: View vultures feeding in the town of Alquézar, Spain

Don't Miss

→ Feeling a spine-tingling shiver at a vulture's screech

→ Witnessing vultures spin high into the sky on a thermal

→ Ticking off passing migrants birds, such as common cranes, black and white storks, ospreys and black kites.

There's something so grotesque about vultures as to make them utterly fascinating. They spend hours at a time gliding effortlessly on thermals, but when they find a carcass, any grace they had in the air is gone. In argumentative groups, they stretch their long necks deep into the unfortunate creatures' insides to get at tasty morsels, their feathers caked in blood. Forget owls; the griffon vultures of the Pyrenees are the ultimate Halloween birds!

Migration corridor

The western end of the Pyrenees is one of Europe's hot-spots for griffon vultures. It seems that you only have to glance up at the sky to see one whirling past – so close you can hear the wind rushing through their outstretched wing feathers. There are many places in the western Pyrenees to spot griffon vultures, but the domed (and easy to hike) summits rising from the Iraty forests are one of the best.

It's not just griffon vultures you'll see here. The mountains are home to growing populations of bearded vultures (lammergeier) and Egyptian vultures, as well as booted eagles, giant golden eagles and black and red kites by the hundred.

Iraty also lies under a major migration route for thousands of birds heading from Northern Europe to Africa. Whether you're captivated or disturbed by the sight of vultures, it's an exceptional place to enjoy the birdlife of the Pyrenees!

Find Your Joy

Getting there
The Iraty region's birdwatching hub is the Chalets d'Iraty, with a bird-info centre open Easter to late October. The chalets are a 1½-hour (53-mile/85km) drive from Biarritz airport; there's no public transport. At nearby Col d'Organbidexka, expert birders are on hand, with scopes and binoculars for public use during the migration seasons. The two nearest places with tourist facilities are Saint-Jean-Pied-de-Port and Larrau.

Accessibility
There aren't really any dedicated facilities for wheelchair users or other birdwatchers with mobility impairments, but you can park right next to the Col d'Organbidexka and watch passing vultures and other birds from the comfort of your vehicle.

When to go
Vultures and other raptors can be seen year-round. Visit in April to May and September to October to see migrating birds passing through.

Further information
• Free admission.
• Open year-round.
• Chalets d'Iraty has food and accommodation; book ahead.
• www.chalets-iraty.com

© AlbertoGonzalez / Shutterstock; tolobalaquer.com / Shutterstock

Other Pyrenees Vulture-Watching Sites

Escuaín Gorge, Spain

Three spectacular Aragon canyons spin off the southern slopes of Mont Perdu (Perdido). The smallest and least-known among humans is the narrow Escuaín Gorge in the east of the park, but vultures found the sheer, secluded cliff faces to their liking long ago. A short and easy hike to the observation platforms is almost guaranteed to result in sightings of bearded vultures.

Don't miss
Other raptors swooping by, such as griffon vultures and golden eagles.

Sierra de Guara, Spain

Dropping off the southern slopes of the high Pyrenees in Aragon, the lower, hotter, drier Sierra de Guara is renowned for its huge numbers of vultures and other raptors. In some places, such as just outside of the pretty village of Alquézar, a vulture feeding station has been established, and once or twice a week hundreds of vultures can be observed at close quarters.

Don't miss
The gruesome but fascinating spectacle of vultures feasting.

Suffolk, England

Hear the boom of bitterns in the marshes at Minsmere

 Migratory visitors, views, connection with nature

 February to June

Sometimes the joy of birding can be crystalised as a simple sound, breaking the almost-silence on a still morning beneath endless, washed-out skies scented with chlorophyll and sea brine.

Whether or not you spot the maker of that mysterious resonance among the reeds is almost academic. It's the lack of other noises to distract you from these hypnotic soundwaves – the absence of mobile-phone ringtones, revving car engines, battling basslines, human chitchat – that makes the magic.

Putting aside the love of lists and long lenses, birding is 25% scientific investigation, 25% natural curiosity, 25% thrill-of-the-chase and 25% meditation. It's the meditation part that comes to the fore at RSPB Minsmere, where whispering grasses create orchestral overtures as breezes blow in from the North Sea.

A quiet place

Minsmere is quiet – and we mean that in the best way. Visitors abound but most of them are seasonal, feathered and flighty, leaving the scattered hides dotted around the reedbeds and lagoons to birders who appreciate calm. This isn't a place you come just to spot birds – it's a place to sit and let your alpha waves settle for two or three peaceful hours.

But there are big prizes for birders seeking rare encounters: the marshes provide a seasonal home

Right: A winter murmuration of starlings swirls over Minsmere

Below: Bitterns stalk fish and amphibians at Minsmere reserve

Q&A

What is it about bitterns?
Bitterns are difficult to see but no other bird makes a call like the male in spring. Their booming carries across the reedbeds and the excitement in a hide when a bird comes out into the open or takes a long and rather ponderous flight is palpable.

What's the Minsmere experience?
Peace, quiet, variety, passionate visitors happy to share their knowledge with beginners, a shop selling everything for bird enthusiasts!

How do I get the best from a trip?
Come early and take your time. This is one of the few places in Britain where a 'day list' of 100 species is a strong possibility – but remember to enjoy the bird behaviour as much as the ticking-off of species!

Annette Salkeld, RSPB North Suffolk Coast Reserves warden

© Eric Isselee / Shutterstock; Colin Edwards Wildside / Shutterstock; William Kuhl Photographs / Shutterstock; Anne Elizabeth Mitchell / Shutterstock

for two-tone avocets, bearded tits, graceful marsh harriers, nightjars, nightingales and more. And the bark of rutting red stags adds to Minsmere's unique soundtrack from October to November. But it's the bittern who takes centre stage on this waterlogged section of coastline.

All about that bass

Camouflaged to match the reeds, with darts of buff, ochre and umber, this springtime guest is heard as often as seen, with the 'boom' of the bittern providing an unmistakable bass section for Minsmere's morning chorus.

And what a bass section! The bittern's call is right at the edge of audible sound – imagine the wind blowing over an empty beer bottle, stuck upright in the mud at low tide; or the sound of a vintage brandy glugging from a decanter behind a velvet curtain...

Should you be lucky enough to see a bittern in the process of booming, the spectacle is even

Right: Minsmere is also home to vulnerable marsh harriers

Far right: A windmill at Cley marshes

Overleaf: A wren sings at Minsmere

more remarkable. The top half of the bird seems to inflate to twice its size, as the bittern gulps in air in preparation for its next broadcast. And the louder and bassier the better, as female bitterns prefer gents with big booms.

But don't take seeing (or hearing) a bittern for granted. Even in a good year, the reedbeds at Minsmere may be home to as few as eight booming males. Your best chances of catching a glimpse or a boom are first thing in the morning, when the air has a tangible chill and the reedbeds are draped in milky sheets of mist.

Don't Miss

→ **The boom of the bittern,** resounding through the reeds

→ **Other Minsmere** characters, such as dignified avocets and agile marsh harriers

→ **Visting early in the** morning to enjoy the silence of the reedbeds

Find Your Joy

Getting there
Minsmere is best approached by car, turning off the A12 near Westleton, between Ipswich and Lowestoft. Alternatively, a special bus service runs on demand from Monday to Saturday to meet trains at tiny Darsham station (on the Ipswich–Lowestoft line).

Accessibility
Most of the trails to hides and viewing points are accessible to wheelchair users and others with reduced mobility. Hides have also been designed with wheelchair users in mind.

When to go
The booming season starts in late February – a cold time for early starts on the marshes – and runs through till mid-May, but sightings are easier in June, when females venture out to gather food for growing chicks.

Further information
• Admission charge, free to RSBP members.
• Year-round, except 25 and 26 December.
• Hides available; the visitor centre can supply binoculars.
• Cafe on-site.
• Good seaside accommodation nearby in Southwold.
• www.rspb.org.uk

Other East Anglian Coastal Hot-spots

Cley Marshes, Norfolk

Shifting reeds and mudflats back the beautiful sandy beaches of north Norfolk, creating a delightfully atmospheric setting for encounters with everything from bitterns to bearded reedlings. The reserve at Cley Marshes is well set up for birders, with a cute cafe and six hides, four accessible via boardwalks.

Don't miss

A rewarding afternoon of birding, with a portable lunch assembled at Picnic Fayre and the Cley Smokehouse in Cley-next-the-Sea.

RSPB Snettisham, Norfolk

North of King's Lynn and the royal residence at Sandringham, this estuarine reserve is a haven for waders of all shapes and sizes, from plovers and oystercatchers to godwits and curlews. The flooded gravel pits were excavated to make concrete for bomber runways during WWII, but today, the flightpath is dominated by diverse bird species.

Don't miss

Hypnotic flocks of knots and oystercatchers rising along the shoreline.

© Erni / Shutterstock

Observe the romances and rivalries of Westfjords puffins

 Colourful birds, mating habits, untamed coastlines

 May to mid-August

ICELAND

As you hike to the cliffs hemming Iceland's Westfjords, you might hear a strange melody. With every step, it gets louder and more frenzied, crescendoing into a chorus of chirrups and reproachful grunts. That's when you see them: Atlantic puffins.

For most of the year, these distinctive birds stay at sea, far out of human sight; they bob in the waves, wheel above the midnight-coloured water and dive at speeds of 60mph (97km/h) to scoop up their next beakful of sprats.

But between May and mid-August, they return to land to form screeching, squabbling, beak-clacking communities on Iceland's sea cliffs – and one of the best spots to see them is Vigur Island, which sits in the inky waters of Ísafjarðardjúp in the Westfjords.

Comedians of the bird world
There's something tragicomic about puffins. Their black-and-white bodies and doe-like eyes give them an air of seriousness, but their orange beaks are clownish and bright. With their waddling gait and cacophonous honks, grunts and squawks, it's no wonder the collective noun is a 'circus of puffins'.

These avian theatrics play out every year at Vigur's puffin colony, which is easily reached on a boat excursion from Ísafjörður. As part of the tour, you'll encounter other birdlife like black guillemots and razorbills.

You'll also meet the island's human residents, a lone family of eider-duck farmers, who'll eagerly show you how they collect eider down, a byproduct of the ducks' annual nesting. But the highlight, of course, is watching puffins at the height of mating season.

Right: Puffins catch fish by diving into the sea, often having flown a great distance

Below: Puffins tend to pair for life and will return to the same burrow each year

Q&A

I'm a novice birdwatcher. Are Iceland's Westfjords for me?
Birding here is relatively easy because you don't have many trees, and most birds are in the sea. There are places in Önundarfjörður and Dýrafjörður to look at wader birds like ringed plover, black-tailed godwits and different ducks feeding on the mudflats.

You've spent years monitoring Icelandic birdlife. Any headlines?
The number of wader birds is increasing. It could be global warming, causing vegetation to advance over the lava fields and increase their habitat. But most seabirds are declining. To learn why, we're monitoring guillemots, razorbills, kittiwakes and Arctic terns, because they're in some kind of danger.

How can I make sure I don't endanger them myself?
Good practice is to never speak loudly and never go close to nests. If you go to an eider duck farm, avoid visiting during nesting time and get permission from the farmer.

Cristian Gallo, ecologist, Natural Science Institute of the Westfjords

© Menno Schaefer / Shutterstock; Alamin-Khan / Shutterstock; Maleo Photography / Shutterstock

Left: An arctic fox in Iceland, predator of puffin chicks

Right: A family of Barrow's goldeneye ducks on Lake Mývatn

Don't Miss

→ **Kayaking from Ísafjörður to see seals and the 'Troll's Seat', Naustahvilft**

→ **Spotting seabirds on a birdwatching boat tour of Ísafjarðardjúp**

→ **Meeting colour-changing canines at nearby Súðavík's Arctic Fox Centre**

Love & loyalty

Starting in May, hundreds of preening puffins descend on Vigur's craggy shores. You'll see them tottering across the lichen-spattered rocks, grunting and clacking in an amorous display.

Their famous curved beaks turn deeper orange in time for mating season. Bachelor puffins use this flash of colour in the hope of luring their forever mate, while longstanding couples greet each other with affectionate beak rubs. Rivalries erupt, too, as puffins clash over the most sheltered nesting spots. It's an almost-human drama, laid out on sea cliffs at the ends of the Earth.

Winged warriors

Other birdlife on Vigur Island doesn't need much seeking out – in fact, some birds might find you instead. Many birdwatchers looking for puffins have been caught unawares by Arctic terns, which dive-bomb unsuspecting humans. Walking tours even kit you out with flags to misdirect lightning-fast tern attacks.

Distinguishable by their black caps, scarlet beaks and mist-grey feathers, these hardy birds have the longest migration route of any creature on the planet, flying more than 43,500 miles (70,000km) between their Nordic summer breeding grounds and South Africa. Their tendency to swoop walkers who get too close to their nests is a reminder: when mating season arrives, Vigur belongs to the birds – everyone else is just passing through.

Find Your Joy

Getting there

Most visitors arrive in Ísafjörður as part of a cruise around Iceland or the Nordics. With close attention to the Westfjords' scant bus timetables, it's possible to get here by public transport, but independent travellers generally hire a car from Reykjavík and drive the winding roads to Ísafjörður. West Tours (www.westtours.is) offers walking tours of Vigur, including the return boat trip from Ísafjörður.

Accessibility

Vigur is unsuitable for wheelchairs due to rocky and uneven walking paths. There are wheelchair-accessible puffin and whale-watching cruises around Skjálfandi Bay from Húsavík, northern Iceland.

When to go

May to mid-August for sociable swarms of puffins and plentiful Arctic terns.

Further information

• Admission charge; reserve ahead.
• Open May to August.
• No specialist facilities.
• Restaurants in Ísafjörður: try Tjöruhúsið's seafood buffet or Heimabyggð's cake/open sandwiches.
• Accommodation in Ísafjörður and Bolungarvik.
• www.vigurisland.com

© Puspok / Shutterstock; Arterra Picture Library / Alamy Stock Photo

Other Icelandic Bird Havens

Lake Mývatn

Avoid the summertime midges at this northern lake by visiting in late April and May, when myriad birds come to feed on the midge larvae: including tufted ducks, red-breasted merganser and dramatically black, white and crimson harlequin ducks. Stop at Sigurgeir's Bird Museum for a lowdown, then head to bird-rich Mývatn bays like Neslandavík and Álar.

Don't miss
Flowing from Mývatn's west side, the Laxá River is the country's best place to spot the rare Barrow's goldeneye.

Vestmannaeyjar

This volcanic archipelago off Iceland's southwest coast is home to Europe's largest puffin colony. Birdwatching tours of main island Heimaey lead to a hide in Stórhöfði, where you can watch puffins clown around. Even better, join a small-boat tour to enter wave-smashed sea caves, while gulls, kittiwakes and murres wheel above.

Don't miss
The 1-mile (1.6km) hike up Eldfell, which erupted on Heimaey in 1973; in some places, the ground is still hot enough to bake bread.

Make way for the great bustard on the Nagyalföld prairie

 Rural isolation, superlative species, connection with nature

 Year-round; sightings difficult July–August

HUNGARY

Witnessing the takeoff of the great bustard on Hungary's Nagyalföld (Great Plain) is both breathtaking and unbelievable. That a bird of such gargantuan proportions can even manage to get off the ground seems a miracle, but this enormous prairie of cropland and grassland, stretching for hundreds of miles east and southeast of Budapest, is a generous runway.

Great bustards are strong fliers and, with a lot of noisy flapping on the otherwise silent plain, they can reach speeds of up to 60mph (100km) after takeoff. And the landing of this fat fellow is almost comical, recalling to birders of a certain provenance the old US television cartoon character Baby Huey, a massively overweight duck whose clumsiness and mammoth size leads him into a series of misadventures.

Bustard basics
The great bustard (Otis tarda) is a goose-like bird weighing in at between 22lb and 44lb (10kg to 20kg), measuring up to 3ft (1m) tall and with wingspan of more than 6.5ft (2m). One of the world's weightiest flying birds, it's the heaviest European land bird that's capable of taking to the air. There are sizeable communities in several countries of Western Europe, but Hungary's endangered population of 1300 birds is the largest in Central and Eastern Europe.

Adult males are a richly mottled golden brown above and

Right: A great bustard in Hungary's Körös-Maros National Park

Below: Although Europe's heaviest birds, great bustards can get airborne, thanks to huge wings

Q&A

Where can I find bustards?
Everyone wants to see a great bustard but for such a big bird, individual sightings can be elusive. You have to know exactly which fields they frequent. This is where a guide comes in.

Is the great bustard the holy grail of birding here?
The great bustard may be the national bird, but Spain and Portugal are full of them, too. The saker falcon and eastern imperial eagle are Asiatic birds that reach Europe uniquely via the Carpathian Basin – Hungary is the best place to see them in the world.

Isn't that the saker falcon on the 'tail' of Hungary's 50Ft coin?
Yes, and its reputation now goes even further. An ornithologist friend wanted to gain more protection for birds of prey here, so he circulated the idea that the mythological turul, the sacred bird of the ancient Hungarians, was in fact the saker falcon. Like the turul, the saker has now become totemic.

Gerard Gorman, ProBirder guide and author of The Birds of Hungary

© Repina Valeriya / Shutterstock; iliuta goean / Shutterstock; Matyas Arvai / Shutterstock; Wim Hoek / Shutterstock

white below, with a grey head and moustache-like tufts. The much smaller female is drabber and less finely marked. Both sexes have long legs and necks, and heavy, barrel-chested bodies. Their gait is slow, deliberate, almost regal. Indeed, with their beaks pointing upward and tail feathers fluffed, they look a little like a queen who kept her crown but donned a tutu for a country stroll. Less attractive is their call – a seldom-heard deep grunt or bark.

Finding bustards in the fields

Great bustards generally feed and nest in crops like barley and oilseed rape, so they can be hard to spot. Mating usually takes place on the open plain in spring and involves a flamboyant display called a lek, when the male competes for the attention of the female, with white tail feathers flared and whiskery chin-feathers pointing straight upward.

The species is very localised and, while there are small and

Right: European rollers migrate through Hungary

Far right: A Eurasian spoonbill, hunting successfully in Hungary

endangered populations in the western part of Hungary, most are found in the east, on the Great Plain. The magnet here for the great bustard has always been the Hortobágy, a vast saline prairie suitable only for grazing. Largely given over to a national park, the Hortobágy is the most birdwatched area in all of Hungary. But it's 2½ hours from Budapest. A more accessible place to see great bustards is Kiskunság National Park, just an hour south of the capital; head for the northern area around the village of Apaj.

Don't Miss

→ Scanning the skies for the arrival of the colossal great bustard

→ Following the slow, deliberate strut of this regal bird

→ Catching a lek, a male's ceremonial advances on a female

Find Your Joy

Getting there
The village of Hortobágy, at the centre of its namesake national park, is accessible by bus and train from Debrecen; the central visitor centre provides park passes. Rte 33 provides access to key sites. Apaj, at the northern edge of Kiskunság National Park, has a study trail and is accessible by bus from Budapest; the closest train station is at Dömsöd.

Accessibility
Trails in the two national parks are generally not accessible for wheelchairs and those with mobility issues.

When to go
Great bustards can be spotted year-round. High vegetation makes birds hard to see in July and August.

Further information
• Free to visitors; passes required for some protected areas in Hortobágy National Park.
• Open year-round.
• Hides available in both national parks.
• Places to eat in Hortobágy and Apaj; most visitors overnight in Debrecen and Budapest.
• www.hnp.hu/en
• www.knp.hu/en

© imageBROKER.com / Shutterstock; Martin Mecnarowski / Shutterstock

Other Hungarian Bird Sites

Bükk National Park

The Bükk Hills, named for the many *bükk* (beech trees) growing here, are a green lung buffering Eger and the industrial city of Miskolc in northeast Hungary. The national park, covering more than 166 sq miles (430 sq km), is a great spot to see four eagle species and eight types of woodpeckers.

Don't miss

April – the best month for woodpeckers and also when the saker falcon and imperial eagle return from the Great Plain to breed.

Fertő-Hanság National Park

In the northwest corner of the country is Lake Fertő, a shallow and brackish body of water that lies mostly in Austria, where it's called Neusiedler See. The lake is celebrated for its waterfowl – herons, spoonbills and egrets can be spotted in this 96 sq mile (250 sq km) national park. April to June sees the most activity in the lake's reedbeds, while August brings white and black storks migrating south.

Don't miss

Visiting in autumn, as thousands of white-fronted and bean geese arrive on passage.

Be mesmerised by swooping swifts in Selborne

 Exuberant swifts, summer evenings, village life

 May to August

Scything through the skies of southern England, whistling to each other in excitement, swifts (apus apus) are a sign that summer has arrived. Every year they fly all the way from Africa and across Europe to the villages of England, where, like countless previous generations, they return to favoured nesting spots to raise their young. Then, as suddenly as they arrived, one day around the start of August they migrate southward once more and the skies of rural England fall silent.

One place where you're guaranteed to see swifts hunting in groups for insects high above the ground is the village of Selborne in northeast Hampshire. The village is typical of many in southern England, with a mix of pretty cottages and modern homes, a pub (and new taproom), a 12th-century church, and a network of footpaths leading into the surrounding countryside. But it has a notable resident in its history: Gilbert White, an 18th-century clergyman regarded as Britain's first naturalist.

Life on the wing

Larger and with plainer plumage than smart, white-breasted swallows, the swift is designed for fast, long-distance flight. Powerful blade-like wings and a blunt, streamlined head help it soar through the air with minimum effort. Famously, the birds spend their whole life in the air, only touching terra firma while incubating their eggs in nests that are often attached to the underside of the eaves of old

Right: Swifts in twilight flight; the Zig Zag Path, cut by Gilbert White's brother

Below: Selborne village from Selborne Common

My Birding Joy

Swifts have a magical power. It's not the ability to fly non-stop from Africa to Northern Europe and live their life entirely on the wing, astonishing though that feat is. Rather, it's how they can slow down time as soon as you stop and watch their arcing flight in the golden light of a summer evening. From the month of May, I listen out for the first squeaky shrieks as the swifts arrive in southern England. They pair up, nest and raise the next generation of superlative fliers over the next three or four months. Selborne has long been favoured by swifts thanks to an abundance of old buildings. But even in 1787 Gilbert White noted that they hadn't bred in great numbers since the church's eaves had been repaired. Today, there are bespoke swift boxes beneath the church roof. As playful groups chase insects and each other, twisting and swooping in an expression of pure freedom, the joy of sharing the summer with the swifts is all the more precious for being so fleeting.

© Gallinago_media / Shutterstock; Robin Barton; skrotov / Shutterstock; Robin Barton

houses. They eat, sleep and drink on the wing. If that's the case, some of you might wonder, then how do they procreate? Gilbert White was the first person to observe the answer. 'If any person would watch these birds of a fine morning in May,' he wrote in his *The Natural History of Selborne*, they would see, every now and then, 'one drop on the back of another and both of them sink down for many fathoms with a loud piercing shriek'.

White's account of the natural life of this parish – its seasons, the comings and goings of the wildlife and dramas large and small – is, as biographer Richard Mabey puts it: 'one of the most perfectly realised celebrations of nature in the English language.'

What to see in Selborne

Selborne is clustered along both sides of a busy B-road, in the shadow of a ridge of steep, wooded hills, known as 'hangers' in this part of Hampshire. On the

Right: The Wakes, former home of naturalist Gilbert White

Far right: A Darwin's finch in the Galapagos archipelago

west side of the road is Gilbert White's house and gardens, The Wakes, now open to the public and offering insights into his life and times. You don't need to hike into the hills to see swifts, although White's brother cut a pathway up the hangers behind his house that is known as the Zig Zag. Swifts much prefer circling above village gardens, chasing each other in the warm evening light. Across the road from The Wakes, is Selborne's church, where there are several benches from where you can admire their acrobatics.

Don't Miss

➜ **Listening for the whistles and shrieks of the swifts in summer**

➜ **Walking up the Zig Zag path for a view over the village**

➜ **Spotting butterflies in the meadows of the Common**

Find Your Joy

Getting there
The nearest train station is Alton, about 6 miles (10km) to the north of Selborne. Alton is on a direct rail line from London Waterloo. A bus service passes through the village a couple of times a day.

Accessibility
Portable hearing loops are located at Gilbert White's House. The ground floor of the house, the cafe and the gift shop have level or ramped access but there is no lift to the second floor. There is level access to the Garden for those with mobility difficulties. Accessible toilets are available.

When to go
To see swifts, expect their arrival in England in May and for them to depart during early August. Some years are better than others.

Further information
• Admission charge to Gilbert White's House but no charge to walk around the churchyard.
• The House is open year-round.
• Dogs welcome on a lead around the wider estate. Cyclists are also welcome.
• Cafe on-site.
• www.gilbert-whiteshouse.org.uk

Other Naturalists' Birds

Darwin's finches, Galapagos

As innocuous as they appear, the modestly plumaged finches of the Galapagos islands played a big part in our understanding of human evolution. Charles Darwin, on his travels through the Ecudorian archipelago on HMS *Beagle*, noticed that the beaks of the finches on each island had each adapted in a slightly different way, according to the foods available.

Don't miss

The small ground finch is widespread across the Galapagos.

Sparrowhawks, England

British naturalist Chris Packham has done a lot for birds around the world, for example by campaigning against the annual bird shoots in Malta. But his favourite bird is most readily seen zipping through English gardens. The sparrowhawk, as its name suggests, preys on the small birds of our suburbs. 'I like the idea of supporting the whole food chain,' says Packham.

Don't miss

A sparrowhawk dive-bombing a bird table.

Oceania

© GPNaturePhotos / Alamy Stock Photo

Climb into the canopy with Bruny Island's forty-spotted pardalotes

 Endemic species, rare sightings, prehistoric plants

 August to December

AUSTRALIA

An island off an island, Tasmania is home to an astoundingly diverse array of wildlife – and if you're after a greatest-hits compilation in a compact space, you can't do much better than 140-sq-mile (362-sq-km) Bruny Island, easily accessible from Hobart. In addition to rare white wallabies, it's home to all 12 of Tasmania's endemic bird species, including the dusky robin, the green rosella and the endangered forty-spotted pardalote.

Passerine paradise

Bruny's Inala Private Conservation Reserve encompasses 1500 acres (600 hectares) of wet eucalypt woodland, heathlands and wetlands, and has an impressive Jurassic Garden showcasing over 750 species that trace their ancestral roots to the Gondwana supercontinent. When Inala was founded some 30 years ago, there were just a handful of pint-sized pardalotes here – but the reserve has cultivated such an inviting atmosphere that it's now perhaps the best place in the world to see these diminutive passerines.

The tiniest and easiest to miss of the dozen endemic pardalote species, forty-spotteds weigh about as much as 10 paperclips and are restricted to an increasingly smaller corner of southeastern Tasmania – most notably on Bruny and Maria Islands – where they live among manna gum trees.

Tasmania's tiny farmers

With a greenish-grey body and a yellow head, forty-spotted pardalotes are identifiable by their namesake markings, which look as if they've been meticulously applied with a fine paintbrush. They're the kind of birds that

Right: A nesting box for pardalotes in Inala Private Conservation Reserve on Bruny Island

Below: A close-up of a forty-spotted pardalote on Bruny Island, they're about 4in (10cm) long

Q&A

What makes pardalotes special?
They're ridiculously tiny and sometimes flutter more like a butterfly than a bird. I find them very sweet to watch in their busy shenanigans, impossible not to admire.

Any tips for first-timers?
Once you've seen their darting and dancing flight patterns, you will notice each time they stop, the leaves shake in a characteristic sharp way that catches the eye. A pair of binoculars is essential, as they are often high in the canopy – be prepared to get a bit of a sore neck.

How does it feel to spend time with Inala's pardalotes?
It is always a smile-cracking delight to watch them thriving and to know that every new chick is so vital for keeping the species alive. To watch them so close by with the naked eye fills my heart to overflowing.

Cat Davidson, Inala Nature Tours guide

AUSTRALIA 60c

Forty-spotted Pardalote *Pardalotus quadragintus* 2013

© Jeremy Edwards / Getty Images; Jen Watson / Shutterstock; Chris Dorney / Alamy Stock Photo

Left: A wild Bennett's wallaby peeks through the bush

Right: Cape Barren geese have colonised a former convict station on Maria Island

themselves and their chicks.

Up close with pardalotes

Tiny forty-spotted pardalotes are often difficult to see, as they spend so much time high up in the canopy. To increase your chances, Inala has installed a 13ft (4m)-high viewing platform among the branches, allowing face-to-beak views of these industrious birds. You can witness them feasting not only on manna but also lerp, a sugary substance exuded by sap-sucking insects that hardens into a protective 'candy bunker' and provides a tasty treat for pardalotes.

Of course, none of this would be possible without the tireless efforts of the Inala team, who are planting manna gums and installing nest boxes to mimic the increasingly scarce hollows in mature gum trees that pardalotes require to raise their chicks. These days, Inala more than lives up to the Aboriginal meaning of its name: 'a peaceful place'.

Don't Miss

➜ Traipsing through a garden of prehistoric plants from Gondwanaland

➜ Catching sight of the island's famed white wallabies

➜ Spotting wedge-tailed eagles and white goshawks from Inala's raptor hide

inspire pilgrimages for checklist-obsessed birders, but you're missing out if you don't take time to observe them as they work.

Forty-spotteds are one of the few bird species that can be considered 'farmers', in that they modify their landscape to harvest nutrients. Using a hook at the end of their stubby beaks, they puncture young eucalyptus shoots, causing sap to ooze from the incision. They then wait for their 'crop' to be ready – in this case, the sap crystallises into manna, an edible resin – before returning to harvest the spoils for

Find Your Joy

Getting there
From Tasmania's capital, Hobart, drive about 30 minutes south to Kettering for the quick

car ferry to Bruny Island. From the ferry terminal, it's about a 45-minute drive south to Inala. There's a fee to access the nature museum and botanic garden; to use the pardalote viewing platform or access the rest of the property, you must stay onsite or book a tour. Hourly fees apply also for the raptor photography hide.

Accessibility
The Jurassic Garden has wheelchair-friendly paths. The pardalote-viewing platform is only accessible via stairs; bring binoculars to increase the likelihood of spotting pardalotes from ground level.

When to go
Go between August and December, during the breeding season.

Further information
• Admission charge.
• Open year-round.
• Hide and viewing platform available.
• Bruny Island has abundant places to sample local produce.
• Inala has on-site cottages and a nearby beachfront rental.
• www. inalanaturetours. com.au

© Andrew Balcombe / Shutterstock; Shutterstock; AngryBirdProductions / Shutterstock

Other Bird-Rich Islands off Tasmania

Maria Island National Park

The plentiful wombats get top billing at this former penal settlement, but today's car-free 'Tasmanian Eden' is also home to a flourishing colony of introduced Cape Barren geese. They're recognisable by their bubblegum-pink legs and highlighter-yellow cere (the skin above the beak), and share the mountainous island with parrots, plovers, pardalotes and more.

Don't miss

Booking a multiday island hike with Great Walks of Australia.

Flinders Island

This largest of the Furneaux Islands, in the Bass Strait between Tasmania and mainland Australia, is home to a wide variety of seabirds, including albatrosses, petrels and gulls. Particularly noteworthy are the short-tailed shearwaters, known here as muttonbirds and a traditional source of protein in these parts. (If you're wondering, they taste like fishy chicken.)

Don't miss

Watching massed shearwaters return to their burrows at dusk from the Settlement Point Viewing Platform.

Witness the whio: a blue duck that whistles

♡ Remote mountains, unique birds, adventure

🕐 November to January

NEW ZEALAND

While you're sure of seeing a whio, or blue duck if you flip over a New Zealand $10 note and check out the bird on the back, there's a decent chance of spotting a pair in the wild too, particularly while walking the world-renowned Milford Track in the South Island's Fiordland National Park.

No ordinary duck

The slate-blue whio, endemic to Aotearoa, is no ordinary quacking duck. It's a mountain duck, living on fast-flowing rivers at altitude, the male emitting the high-pitched wheezy whistle – 'whi-o!' – from which the Māori derived its name.

While the male whistles, the female growls: fiercely territorial whio are monogamous,

mate for life, and claim rights to one mile (1.6km) or more of river per couple.

Sleek swimmers, they battle through whitewater rapids and dive beneath fast-flowing water in search of food, using their soft bill – tipped with a lip-like membrane – to roll underwater rocks and uncover larvae of aquatic insects, such as caddisfly, stonefly and mayfly.

The curse of introduced predators

Spotting a whio while walking the Milford Track is an absolute thrill, a highlight for any bird enthusiast and likely to match the natural high brought on by the stupendous alpine scenery. This is Fiordland: towering, steep-sided glacial-carved valleys, with rushing

Right: The plumage of both sexes of whio is quite similar; male heads may be more green

Below: Whio hunt for freshwater invertebrates in fast-flowing waterways

Q&A

What's to love about whio?
The whio is a 'duck with attitude'! They're really feisty, even the ducklings. I love that they're an ancient species scrapping for survival, when the modern world is threatening their extinction. And I love working in their stunning mountain habitat. There's no better office in the world.

How many whio on the Milford Track?
We're up to 60 breeding pairs, possibly more, along the Milford Track and its tributary valleys. Corporate sponsors fund Department of C onservation to help eradicate introduced predators through trapping. I find it extremely satisfying that we can not only save endangered birds like the whio, but increase their numbers.

Tips for spotting whio?
Stay alert near fast water. Whio will see you before you see them. The male will whistle, so you'll know they're around.

Max Smart, Te Anau Department of Conservation senior ranger

© Eric Isselee / Shutterstock; Hot Pixels Photography / Shutterstock; Molly Marshall / Alamy Stock Photo; Nui Rattapon / Shutterstock

rivers fed by melting snow and glaciers – and 23ft (7m) of rainfall per year!

Before the arrival of the stoat, brought by Europeans in 1879 to control numbers of introduced rabbits, nesting on the ground by a river was not a problem for the whio. Nowadays, though, adult birds, eggs and ducklings are at the mercy of this voracious, bird-killing little mustelid, notorious as the worst of the introduced predators.

But the whio is getting help to fight back. Thanks to intense stoat-trapping by the Department of Conservation (DoC), whio numbers throughout the country are on the rise, estimated at around 3000 birds.

Whio on the Milford Track

With around 60 breeding pairs, the Milford Track is an excellent place to search out the whio. On this famous, 33-mile (53km) trail, labelled the 'finest walk

Right: Lake Quill and Sutherland Falls near Milford Sound

Far right: Hiking the Routeburn Track above Lake Mackenzie

in the world' by the *London Spectator* over 100 years ago, it's relatively easy to get into remote mountain country.

To be in with a chance of spotting a whio while you walk, you'll need to keep your eyes open and ears tuned. Ever alert, whio scan the whitewater. Observing whio rafting by in the rapids is a trail highlight, always the talk of the day among hikers, guides and hut wardens come the evening, once settled into huts and lodges. A whio sighting is one to be savoured.

Don't Miss

→ The shrill warning call of the male whio when it detects you are near

→ Walking to the base of the 1900ft-high (580m) Sutherland Falls

→ Listening to birdcalls, such as that of the kiwi, after dark

Find Your Joy

Getting there
The Milford Track is accessed from the town of Te Anau. The only way onto and off the track is by boat;

there are daily departures during these months.

Accessibility
Wheelchair users will have difficulty getting on and off the boats used to access both ends of the Milford Track. The first and last bits of the trail are flat, however, and can be enjoyed by those with limited mobility as part of a day-visit, such as

with Trips & Tramps (www.tripsandtramps.com).

When to go
The Milford Track hiking season runs from the start of November to late April. Independent hikers can book online through the Department of Conservation, guided walkers through Ultimate Hikes (www.ultimatehikes.co.nz). Whio can be

seen on the water with ducklings from November to January.

Further information
• November to late April.
• Guided 5-day/4-night walks cost from NZ$2595.
• DoC huts charge overnight fees of NZ$78 per night.
• www.doc.govt.nz

Other South Island Whio Habitats

Routeburn Valley, Mt Aspiring National Park

Accessible from Queenstown by car, bus or on a guided day-walk, the Routeburn Valley – also home to a world-renowned multiday hiking track – is a good place to spot whio. The fast-flowing Routeburn River is ideal whio habitat, and DoC has helped out by trapping predators both here and in neighbouring valleys.

Don't miss

The whitewater rapids around Forge Flat, about one hour's walk up the valley from the car park.

Monkey Creek, Fiordland National Park

You can seek out whio sightings in relative ease on the Te Anau to Milford Sound highway, 58 miles (94km) from Te Anau at Monkey Creek. Named after the dog of an early European settler (there are no monkeys in Aotearoa), the creek enters the Hollyford River at a large flat here, beneath the towering walls of the glacier-carved valley.

Don't miss

Stunning views up the valley of Mt Talbot.

Admire the alfresco architecture of great bowerbirds

Eccentricity, enthusiastic exhibitionism, eclectic collections

August to October

AUSTRALIA

In his much-quoted *Locksley Hall*, Tennyson wrote that 'In the Spring a young man's fancy lightly turns to thoughts of love' – and come spring in the southern hemisphere, hormonal male great bowerbirds have this (if not much else) in common with the poem's lovelorn youth. Imagine, perhaps, a long arcade of trees in a formally landscaped garden, hinting at a promise of what lies ahead; then transpose this image to a crackling patch of dry-season bush in Australia's Northern Territory where, at knee-height, a precision-designed tunnel with beautifully woven stick-walls has been painstakingly constructed. Roughly 20in (50cm) wide and 23in (60cm) long, this is a great bowerbird's bower, and it's asking to be noticed.

But it's not only size that's important to the bowerbird: both exterior and interior decoration reflect an individual bowerbird's personal idiosyncrasies. One of Australia's several species of delightfully bonkers bower-builders, great bowerbirds are huge fans of grey, white and green – with the occasional nod to pink – and they decorate the entrance and exit foyers, as well as the floor of the bower itself, with many sundry scavenged objects.

Reduce, reuse, recycle
Bowerbirds' collections are eclectic, from shells and seeds to clothes pegs, ring-pulls from cans, dull glass or shiny syringes. These are often pilfered in public from the picnic tables, ablution blocks and tent sites of unwary campers or from backyard washing lines. Placement in the bower is obsessively considered and intentional: alter the decor

Right: Bowerbird habitat in Kakadu National Park in the Northern Territory

Below: Two young great bowerbirds practise their building skills and collecting things

© crbellette / Shutterstock; Catherine Sutherland / Lonely Planet; Marianne Purdie / Shutterstock

Q&A

What's the dress code?
Understated elegance, wearing a business suit of feathers in conservative shades of grey, belied by that secret blaze of punk-pink crest. Definitely dressed to impress.

Your first sighting?
I was living in Kakadu. On a visit to Nawurlandja in February 1994 I wrote in my notebook: 'he's dancing in front of his bower...it's beautifully curated with snail shells, broken clear and green glass, aluminium foil...'. It was love at first sight!

Introvert or extrovert?
Bowerbirds are unfazed by company. At Batchelor School near Darwin, they vie for sweet mango flesh alongside blue-faced honeyeaters, rainbow lorikeets and northern rosellas. The kids call them 'lunch box birds': when the end-of-lunch-it's-time-to-line-up bell rings, bowerbirds gorge on any leftovers they can lay their beaks on.

Kaye Aldenhoven, NT poet, birdwatcher and teacher

Left: The pink crest of male great bowerbirds is used to entice females of the species

Right: An unmistakeable orange-footed scrubfowl

Don't Miss

→ Counting and identifying the bowerbird's collection of found objects

→ Leaving a grey/white/green housewarming gift of leaves or stones

→ Melding into the bush surrounds while waiting for the bower-builder's return

when its builder is not around and he'll move it back where it belongs, quick-smart.

The bower is not a nest – it's more of a speed-dating love shack. A bowerbird introduces himself to a visiting female, flirts a bit, struts his stuff and – if she's interested – they mate, no strings attached. After this point she's on her own and he repeats the process.

Making a song & dance about it
A male bowerbird certainly knows how to draw attention to himself. Watching from the adjacent bush, a quiet observer will likely first notice his strange series of noises – hissings, creakings, snappings. Only the kindest would call these a song.

Then, on tippytoes, with tail fanned and wings stretched, he bounces around the bower. He picks up and shows-off objects while simultaneously dipping his head to reveal an astonishing splash of fluorescent pink-purple on the back of his neck – it's this 'nuchal crest' that gives the bird its scientific name, *Chlamydera nuchalis*.

Looking around, the observer may also spy a silently attentive female, watching and listening to the performance. If she enters the bower for a closer inspection, he plays peekaboo, peeping around the entrance with gifts. If she declines his advances, she will fly away – leaving him literally crestfallen. Anyone who's ever been a clumsy teenager in love may find this behaviour uncannily familiar.

Find Your Joy

Getting there
Kakadu National Park's nearest city is Darwin, on the north–south Stuart Hwy and with international

and domestic airports. Kakadu lies 155 miles (250km) east of the city by road: there's no public transport to the park, so you'll need to have your own car (or rent one in Darwin). Ask at Kakadu's HQ, Bowali Visitor Centre near Jabiru township, for information on active bowers – Ubirr and Gunlom campsites are likely spots.

Accessibility
Most parts of Kakadu are reachable via sealed roads, but getting to bowerbird sites may mean a walk along uneven ground.

When to go
Great bowerbirds are visible all year, but are busiest at their bowers during the late dry season (August to October); come prepared for high temperatures and humidity, and bring insect repellent.

Further information
• Fee for Kakadu park passes.
• Year-round.
• No specialist facilities.
• Supplies, refreshments and accommodation at Jabiru.
• www.parksaustralia. gov.au

© Erni / Shutterstock; Minden Pictures / Alamy Stock Photo

Other Australian Avian Architects

Tooth-billed bowerbirds, Atherton Tablelands

These rainforest minimalists are on the other end of the spectrum of bower-builders. In these North Queensland forests, you might notice a carefully cleared patch of ground: this is a lek, or mating stage, sparsely decorated with fresh leaves, always laid pale underside up. Move or add one and you'll likely prompt an assertive male to fly in and reposition or remove it.

Don't miss
Scrutinising nearby trees for perching males, patiently waiting for females.

Orange-footed scrubfowl, Darwin

Nicknamed 'bush chooks', these ubiquitous mound-builders are frequent visitors to the George Brown Darwin Botanic Gardens. Their heaped mounds of sand and vegetation compost down, creating enough heat to incubate eggs laid inside. Scrubfowl are scientifically known as megapodes, meaning 'big-footed' – follow their noisy scratching to find their mounds, up to 15ft (4.5m) high and 30ft (9m) across.

Don't miss
Taking a good look at the scrubfowl's bright orange feet.

Make a date with a superb fairy-wren in Melbourne

 Living jewels, restful parks and gardens, superb coffee

 Australia's spring and summer

AUSTRALIA

A spark of vivid blue catches your eye. It flits around in staccato movements in the hedge before standing still long enough for you to get a better look at this tiny dynamo. A sky-blue cap sits atop a dark blue cowl, with a flash beneath each eye. The plumage is accessorised with a perky tail and the whole bird could comfortably sit in the palm of your hand. It's a superb fairy wren and it's one of urban Australia's most engaging birds.

The superb fairy-wren is part of the ten-strong *Malurus* family, most of which are widely distributed across Australia. Showy sibling, the splendid fairy-wren is almost entirely an electric blue and backs up its bright plumage with unnecessary bravado by singing mating songs in front of predators. The lovely fairy-wren has delightful chestnut wings, as does the variegated fairy-wren, which has the longer tail if you need to tell between the two. The blue-breasted fairy-wren is concentrated in the southwest of Australia as is the red-winged fairy-wren, which lives among giant karri trees.

But the fairy-wren you're most likely to see in Melbourne and other cities is the superb one. This is because it dwells in the shrubs and dense understorey that you might still find in parks and gardens in the city, using these bushes for cover as it darts out to feed on small insects and seeds. Unlike its siblings, it feeds more frequently at ground level, so keep an eye out low down.

Popularity contest
It has pop-culture presence too, triumphing in Australia's biennial bird-of-the-year poll

Right: The males of the wren family have the brighter plumage

Below: Melbourne's Royal Botanic Gardens features water and trees but not many wrens currently

© trabantos / Shutterstock; wildcyprus / Shutterstock

Q&A

What are your favourite birds to be around in Melbourne's gardens?
I think my favourite bird is the Eastern spinebill. It's a pretty little bird with black, white and chestnut markings with a long black beak. We often see it feeding on the flowers of salvias, abutilons and correas. I also like the Nankeen night heron and the tawny frogmouth, both night birds, but during the day you can see them keeping still and looking secretive.

Aren't Australian birds quite rowdy?
We have lovely sounding birds such as the grey butcher. The little birds, such as the spotted pardalotes and fairy-wrens make sweet chirpy sounds. Perhaps the most liked is the tinkling bell sound of the bell miner, which can be heard all around the lake. But we have noticed that the more aggressive birds are pushing the fairy-wrens out of the gardens and we haven't seen one here for a few years.

Can the garden help the small birds?
If there's more dense planting of undergrowth then maybe the little birds will feel safer.

Liz Cooper, bird walk guide at Melbourne's Royal Botanic Gardens

Right: Street art by Smug feauring a fairy-wren in Frankston

Far right: An Australian magpie in Sydney

organised by *The Guardian Australia* and BirdLife Australia in 2021. Previous winners include the Australian magpie, the black-throated finch and the swift parrot in 2023. But among Melbourne's urban birds, it has stiff competition for most appealing bird. Soft pink and grey galahs stroll across pitches and parks. Sulphur-crested cockatoos shriek and yell. Flocks of rainbow lorikeets speed from tree to tree.

But there's a special sense of joy from seeing something so small, so pretty and so tentative as a fairy-wren. If you sit quietly and watch where you know a group live, it's smile-inducing reward when they pop out and hop around briefly.

And that's the other under-appreciated aspect of looking out for birds in Melbourne. You can do it quite comfortably. You can pick up a flat white from one of Melbourne's countless excellent coffee shops and sit down somewhere suitable for 15 minutes and just be focused on the moment. Let all your thoughts fade into the background and allow your attention to be fully absorbed in what this tiny bird is doing.

Where to find fairy-wrens

Although once seen in Melbourne's Royal Botanic Gardens, the superb fairy-wrens appear to have been bullied out. But they can still be spotted alongside the Yarra and Maribyrnong rivers and in parks and gardens around city.

Don't Miss

→ Walking or cycling the Merri Creek and Yarra River trails

→ Being entranced by a superb fairy wren's busy life

→ Exploring Melbourne's many parks and public gardens that are packed with native plants

Find Your Joy

Getting there
Melbourne is reached by domestic flights from across Australia, trains from Sydney, Canberra and Adelaide, and by international flights. Once in Melbourne, you can get around the city by public transport easily on trams and trains (but there's still no train from the main airport). Buy a Myki travel card for convenience.

Accessibility
Many of Melbourne's most popular public paths and trails that may take you into superb fairy-wren habitat are very accessible. Some, such as the Merri Creek and Yarra Trails are quite wide, paved and level. Tram and train platforms are also relatively accessible, with ramps.

When to go
Although no time is a bad time to visit Melbourne, wrens are most active in spring (from August) and summer when mating and raising broods.

Further information
• No entry fees but birding tours cost $10
• www.rbg.vic.gov.au

Other Australian Urban Birds

Australian magpie

For some of the year, the Australian magpie has a reputation as fearsome as any Melbourne gangland enforcer. When protecting their nests in spring, magpies will behave thuggishly, divebombing passersby and stabbing at them with their powerful beaks and claws. They're highly intelligent birds that will also bear a grudge. But all is forgiven as soon as the magpie starts singing. The warbling carols of these monochrome menaces are completely enchanting.

Don't miss

Magpies can be spied everywhere, particular in parks and gardens, scouring the ground for insects.

Grey-headed flying fox

No, they're not birds. And they're not foxes either. But these large bats deserve an honourable mention because few sights are as evocative of a warm evening in an eastern Australian city, such as Melbourne, Brisbane or Sydney, as a group of grey-headed flying foxes, Australia's largest bats, flapping overhead on their way to feed on fruit trees. Flying foxes have adapted to urban life and in some cities their roosts, or camps, may number in the thousands of individuals (bringing them into conflict with people).

Don't miss

Seeing them along the coastal belt from Melbourne to Rockhampton.

Spot the biggest species of kiwi, the tokoeka

 Flightless birds, screeching birdcalls, rare encounters

 November to March

NEW ZEALAND

An hour south of the mainland by ferry, Stewart Island/ Rakiura – Aotearoa's third-largest island – may have a human population of only 400, but once the sun goes down, an estimated 20,000 kiwi are out there running around, their screeching calls creating a lively natural nightlife. They're easier to hear than to see, though: they tend to shy away from humans, and rarely come close to inhabited areas.

Surviving European predators

Kiwi didn't need to fly before the arrival of humans to these remote Pacific islands, some 800 years ago. Over thousands of years, they evolved into flightless ground-dwellers, with tiny functionless wings and no tail; so when humans eventually turned up, bringing various predators with them, the kiwi was pretty much defenceless. Numbers plummeted, and it would be fair to say that most Kiwis (New Zealanders, that is!) have never seen their national bird in the wild.

However, with no mustelids (stoats and ferrets) on the island of Rakiura, kiwi here have had a much better chance of survival than their mainland cousins, despite the presence of other introduced predators, such as rats and possums.

The joy of the search

Māori consider the kiwi a *taonga* (treasure) and have strong cultural and spiritual associations with the bird. Given this special status, and the elusive nature of kiwi in their natural habitat, spotting a one on a guided tour of Mamaku Point Conservation Reserve is an absolute thrill.

Right: A weka, another of New Zealand's flightless birds, roams the beach

Below: A southern brown kiwi, or tokoeka, forages on pest-free Ulva Island, part of Rakiura National Park

Q&A

Why's the tokoeka so special?

It's our species of kiwi down here and we're proud of it. Even though it's just a fluffy, awkward ball when it emerges from its egg, it can already fend for itself. It's a fighter! I've been here, like...forever, but I still get a huge thrill every time I see one.

The locals love it?

We have our own Stewart Island / Rakiura Community & Environment Trust that all locals support. We have all sorts of programmes. All domestic dogs on Rakiura are encouraged to go through our kiwi-aversion training, which we offer twice a year. Everyone supports the eradication of predators such as rats and possums. And we have a goal to engage the community and visitors in Kiwi conservation.

Ulva Goodwillie, author & owner of Ulva's Guided Walks, Rakiura

© Harvepino / Shutterstock; Kerry Hargrove / Shutterstock; Tomas Pavelka / Shutterstock

Left: The beaches of Stewart Island / Rakiura are prime tokoeka habitat

Right: British Prince William met a kiwi bird when he visited Kāpiti Island

This excitement morphs into a stunned silence as everyone tries to keep quiet in the hope of extending the encounter. Too much noise and the shy, reclusive kiwi will soon disappear into the safety of the dark bush.

Tokoeka or weka?

Rakiura's tokoeka is the largest of the six identified kiwi sub-species; unlike the others, which are nocturnal, the tokoeka is occasionally active during the day. This is probably how it got its name, which means 'weka with a walking stick'. Another flightless bird, the weka is also active by day; you might mistake it for a kiwi should you hear it scratching around the undergrowth in search of food. But the two are easily distinguishable on sight by their bills: kiwi bills are much longer than those of the weka, at up to 8in (20cm) long, with nostrils at the tip – from side-on, the tokoeka does indeed look like a 'weka with a walking stick'.

Don't Miss

➜ The tokoeka male's shrill call answered by the female's sharp screech

➜ Checking out Mamaku Point's impressive predator fence

➜ Post-trip refreshments at Oban's iconic South Sea Hotel

The reserve occupies a 425-acre (172-hectare) peninsula, protected by a 1.3-mile (2.1km) predator fence from Horseshoe Bay to Lee Bay.

Excitement is palpable as kiwi-spotters scramble around using red-light torches in the dark, on steep and uneven ground, through stands of native bush, on muddy tracks, and even on sandy beaches. There's little chance of instant gratification out here!

When visitors do spot a tokoeka, though, it's like finding gold: excitement positively ripples through all those present.

Find Your Joy

Getting there
There are daily ferries (NZ$220 per person) from Bluff, south of Invercargill, to Oban township on Stewart Island/Rakiura, where there's an excellent Department of Conservation (www.doc.govt.nz) Visitor Centre. Mamaku Point (www.mamakupoint.nz) is 3 miles (5km) north of Oban; it's best to visit on a guided tour with Ulva's Guided Walks (www.ulva.co.nz).

Accessibility
Visitors on guided walks need to be able to walk unassisted in the dark for up to two hours; the walks are not suitable for those with visual or hearing impairments or limited mobility, or children under the age of 12.

When to go
Tours operate year-round; the best time to spot tokoeka is after dusk; tours head out at 7pm in winter, 10pm in summer, lasting 2–3 hours, depending on how shy the tokoeka are on the day.

Further information
• Ulva's tours cost NZ$140 per person.
• Year-round.
• There's a good range of accommodation in Oban.
• www.stewartisland.co.nz

© R. Vickers / Shutterstock; Samir Hussein / WireImage / Getty Images

Other Kiwi Places in New Zealand

Zealandia Te Māra a Tāne, Wellington

The world's first fully predator-fenced urban eco-sanctuary, Zealandia is home to some of Aotearoa New Zealand's rarest and most extraordinary wildlife, right in the heart of the capital. While most visitors turn up by day, book a Night Tour online for the opportunity to see some of the 150 little spotted kiwi who live here.

Don't miss
Seeing a plethora of other endangered species on a Zealandia Night Tour.

Kāpiti Island

Kāpiti Island is a predator-free nature reserve off the west coast of the southern North Island, and access is restricted to protect a number of endangered native bird species, many of which have been reintroduced here. Kapiti Island Nature Tours runs overnight trips during which visitors may encounter a little spotted kiwi – there are 1200 on the island.

Don't miss
Bonus spots of nocturnal ruru or morepork (a small brown owl) or a kororā (little blue penguin).

Listen for lyrebirds in Victoria's forests

♡ Enigmatic celebrities, exploring nature, rewarded effort

🕐 June to October

AUSTRALIA

It was British naturalist David Attenborough who introduced much of the rest of the world to Australia's lyrebird. During his 1998 documentary series, *The Life of Birds*, David watched in fascination as a slender, dun-coloured bird in a forest clearing waited for silence before giving a virtuoso vocal performance. It perfectly mimicked a car alarm, a chainsaw, the click of a camera shutter and other human-derived sounds that it had heard in its habitat. This was a virtuoso display designed to impress any potential mates within earshot. Traditionally, the male lyrebird would have replicated the songs of other forest birds but with humans encroaching on their home, the birds had to expand their repertoire.

Showtime
Much of birdwatching isn't actual spotting. It's more about engaging all your senses, with a lot of waiting and good luck. In the case of the lyrebird, there's a lot of listening involved. To maximise your chances, it helps to have a plan: work out where the lyrebirds are likely to be, the type of environment they prefer and when they're at their most gregarious. Winter, from June onwards, is the breeding period for lyrebirds. For six to eight weeks, male lyrebirds will be putting much more vocal effort into their performances, so this is a good time to listen for their songs. They will also seek out a relatively open space, perhaps with some raised ground or a log, to serve as a stage. And then there's

Right: Lyrebirds are not known for their road sense, so drive carefully in their home

Below: A lyrebird in Sherbrooke Forest in the Dandenong Ranges National Park, east of Melbourne

My Birding Joy

The first lyrebird I saw was on television, complete with David Attenborough's customary whispered narration. This was in his 1998 documentary, so I expect that the bird's flawless impression of a camera shutter would today be a copy of the ping of a text message. But I remember being amazed at this bird's strange skills. Australia seemed to have cornered the market in weird and wonderful creatures.

Many years later, when mountain biking in a forest near the alpine town of Bright in northeast Victoria, I noticed a movement through the trees. It was a lyrebird, tentatively sidling out of sight. I paused, hoping it would forget my interruption. Then it hopped up onto a log and started to call, as I stood motionless astride my bike, engrossed in the moment. So what did this lyrebird sound like? Well, almost exactly like R2D2, the droid from the Star Wars movies. I can only assume that it was the call of another forest bird that it was shamelessly ripping off.

© Eric Isselee / Shutterstock; Robert Wyatt / Alamy Stock Photo; K.A.Willis / Shutterstock; FiledIMAGE / Shutterstock

their crowning glory: two curved tail feathers that lend the bird its name (from the Greek musical instrument). These are fanned out to impress any observers.

The lyrebird's range extends from southern Victoria up to New South Wales' border with southeast Queensland. Within a few hours' drive of Melbourne, several national parks have reasonably sized populations where a sighting is quite likely. To the east, the Dandenong Ranges are where David Attenborough filmed his encounter. In addition to the appeal of the lyrebirds here, there's also the *Puffing Billy* Railway that chugs through fern gullies and forest.

Just on the northeast outskirts of Melbourne, the Yarra Ranges are damp forests of mountain ash trees that are also home to a number of amazing animals, including rare Leadbeater's possums, gliders and echidnas. Explore the Yarra Ranges on some of the walking and biking

Right: Book a ride on the *Puffing Billy* steam train in the Dandenongs

Far right: A beautiful Regent honeyeater in New South Wales

Overleaf: Mountain ash trees in Sherbrooke Forest

trails, particularly the O'Shannassy Aqueduct trail that hugs the hills behind the town Warburton and offers plentiful birding opportunities.

And further north is Mt Buffalo, just outside the alpine town of Bright in the High Country. This is mountainous terrain with great granite boulders and a different range of birds to spot, including flame robins. Here, back in the 1920s, local woman Alice Manfield took some of the first photos and films of lyrebirds and published an early nature booklet, *The Lyre-Birds of Mount Buffalo.*

Don't Miss

→ Listening awestruck to a lyrebird's medley of greatest hits

→ Walking some of the tracks through mountain ash forest in the Yarra Ranges

→ Taking a trip back in time on the *Puffing Billy* steam railway in the Dandenongs

Find Your Joy

Getting there
Lyrebirds are present in national parks across the state. Try the Dandenongs, Mt Buffalo or the Yarra Ranges, all of which are most easily reached by car from Melbourne. But it is possible to get to the Yarra Ranges by train and bicycle via Warburton's Rail Trail and to the Dandenongs and Mt Buffalo by train and bus.

Accessibility
Some of the main tracks in the Dandenongs are wheelchair-friendly. But there are fewer options for getting deeper into the Yarra Ranges, and Mt Buffalo is much more rugged.

When to go
The Australian winter, from June onwards for up to eight weeks, is when

male lyrebirds put on their most dramatic displays. But this also coincides with Victoria's coldest and wettest weather. Pack accordingly.

Further information
• Parks are open year-round with no entry fees, although camping overnight costs extra
• www.parks.vic.gov.au

© Catherine Sutherland / Lonely Planet; Henry Cook / Getty Images

Other Rare Aussie Birds

Regent honeyeater

From a bird whose party trick is mimicking others' songs, to a bird that is losing its own songs. There are so few Regent honeyeaters remaining, maybe no more than 300, that they're forgetting the songs they used to sing to each other. Scientists are playing recordings of wild Regent honeyeaters to young birds reared in captivity that will be released as part of a breeding program.

Don't miss

Regent honeyeaters have been sighted at Lake Macquarie in New South Wales and also in a Hunter Valley backyard.

Swift parrot

When Australian birdwatchers chat about Swifties, they're probably talking about the bright green parrot rather than the singer of 'Shake It Off'. Swift parrots are critically endangered birds that breed in Tasmania and migrate across southeast Australia. In a clear case of nominative determinism, they're exceptionally fast flyers. But with the loss of dry woodland habitat to logging and bushfires, they're struggling, reduced to only around 2000 individuals.

Don't miss

Swift parrots feeding on a flowering Tasmanian blue gum, their favourite.

© Gabrielle Sutherland / Lonely Planet

Follow a flutter of bright-blue wings in a Marquesan banana forest

 Endemic species, rare encounters, sense of adventure

 October to December

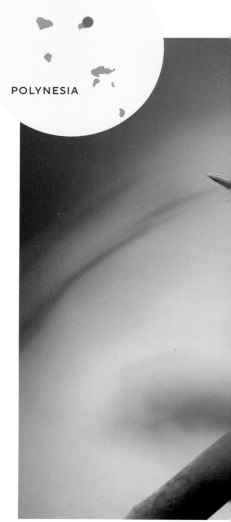

POLYNESIA

Few activities can bring travellers to the furthest corners of the Earth quite like birding. The 32-sq-mile (83-sq-km) volcanic isle of Ua Huka isn't found on most maps, but deep in bands of humid jungle in this otherwise dry, barren landscape hides the rare and endemic ultramarine lorikeet, with plumage so bright blue that it rivals French Polynesia's most dazzling lagoons.

Walking the forested hillside tracks on this idyllic isle, it's easy to understand how the French painter Paul Gauguin was inspired by the hues of the Marquesas Islands. The chartreuse greens and yellows of fan-like banana leaves contrast with the deep, glossy greens of towering mango trees, all reflecting the sky as it turns from azure, to lemon, to pink. You'd think it would be easy to spot an aquamarine and Prussian-blue bird in this palette of warm colours, but guess again: the shadows keep their denizens' secrets.

Nature's magic

But then it happens. A trill of 'piii, piii, pii!' erupts from the forest as a group of small, dark birds – juvenile ultramarine lorikeets, known here as pitihi – flutter the from a banana tree. It's not until they flit through a ray of sunlight that the flash of electric blue on their wings becomes visible. Once you get your eye in, the lorikeets seem to be everywhere, with small flocks alighting from nests hidden in spiky

Right: An ultramarine lorikeet feeding

Below: The unique Ua Huka flycatcher

© kpboonjit / Shutterstock; Michael Greenfelder / Alamy Stock Photo

Q&A

What does seeing the pitihi mean to you?
A connection with nature and the Marquesan culture. Birds are the only land animals endemic to our islands. They were here before us and are a huge part of our identity. Protecting them is paramount.

Tell me more about the cultural part...
Our Haka Manu (bird dance) is the archipelago's signature dance. The people of Ua Huka have created a new choreography for a pitihi dance that we perform at the Marquesas Arts Festivals. It's full of strength, colour and sensuality, much like the bird itself.

How can visitors get the best from a trip?
Take the jungle trail between Hokatu and Hane villages where you'll see not only pihiti, but our other endemics like komako [Marquesan reed warbler] and kuku [white-capped fruit dove].

Chloe Brown, Viaku'a I te Manu o Ua Huka director

Left: Artwork at the Musée Communal de Ua Huka

Right: Sandy beaches and turquoise seas at Rimatara Island in French Polynesia

Don't Miss

→ Scanning mango trees for adult ultramarine lorikeets

→ Listening to myriad seabirds along the coastline

→ Visiting archaeological sites to see ancient tiki sculptures

pandanus trees and ragged coconut palms. Deeper in the shade of the forest, adults might be found resting on low branches.

You may be able to get close enough to see the birds' bright feathers contrasting with their orange beaks and legs in an aesthetically mind-blowing piece of natural design. Here in the middle of the Pacific Ocean, pondering why and how we are gifted this much beauty somehow feels more poignant. It's a setting where nature cannot help but inspire art.

Finding refuge

The ultramarine lorikeet originally hails from the neighbouring islands of Ua Pou and Nuku Hiva, but a schoolteacher brought a pitihi pair to Ua Huka in the 1940s. When shipping docks were built on Ua Pou and Nuku Hiva, the black rat was introduced and quickly eradicated the native lorikeets on both islands, along with many other endemic species. But as Ua Huka's bay is too small for boats to dock, the rats never found their way here and the birds survived. Today two specially trained dogs from New Zealand check over every package that arrives on the island to insure that Ua Huka remains a rat-free sanctuary.

The small, black or brown Ua Huka flycatcher, or pati'oti'o, is another species only found here, and can often be spotted in forested zones, along other birds native to the Marquesas. For birders, it's a rich bounty indeed.

Find Your Joy

Getting there
Ua Huka is served by twice-weekly Air Tahiti flights from Tahiti, via Nuku Hiva. It's also possible to visit Ua Huka on the Aranui V, a mixed cargo/cruise vessel whose owners can arrange birding guides. You can also find local guides on Ua Huka.

Accessibility
Most trails are single-track and not wheelchair accessible, but there are a few spotting sites that are a quick stroll from paved road or are reachable by 4WD.

When to go
Chicks start to emerge in October and you'll see the most action from this time through to December. Sightings depend on unpredictable weather patterns, though, and your chances drop dramatically during droughts and dry periods.

Further information
• Open year-round.
• No specialist facilities.
• Small shops sell sandwiches to pack for lunch.
• Ua Huka has a handful of simple accommodation options.
• www.manu.pf

© robertharding / Alamy Stock Photo; Dmitry Malov / Alamy Stock Photo

Other French Polynesian Birding Hot-spots

Rimatara, Austral Islands

Dotted with flourishing fruit and taro plantations, this pancake-flat 2125-acre (860-hectare) island is characterised by a gracious Polynesian charm; Rimatara is also protected from the black rat, ensuring healthy bird populations. Standout sightings include the Kuhl's lorikeet, an exceptionally bright scarlet, green, blue and yellow bird which has many similar characteristics to the ultramarine lorikeet.

Don't miss

Catching close encounters with Kuhl's lorikeets.

Rapa, Austral Islands

This remote, hard-to-reach subtropical island is home to some 300 endemic bird species, including the Rapa shearwater, which breeds here before migrating to Hawai'l; and the pink and green Rapa fruit dove, found only on this island. There's limited boat-only transportation, so visit on as part of an Aranui V cruise or plan to stay a month or more!

Don't miss

Getting out on a boat to see the Rapa shearwater and endemic petrels along with nine other uncommon sea birds.

Come face to face with a cassowary in Far North rainforests

 Wonder, untamed nature, avian giants

 December to March

AUSTRALIA

Imagine a missing link on the journey from dinosaurs to birds. Now you're ready to meet the southern cassowary, self-styled king of Australia's northern jungles. This enigmatic Australian can be spotted – though not easily – in the dense, dripping rainforests of Far North Queensland, sometimes strutting sedately, sometimes charging through the undergrowth with its fin-like casque (headplate) held down like a battering ram.

Seeing a southern cassowary in its wild habitat depends on a mixture of patience and luck. Perhaps as few as 1000 birds survive in pockets of dense jungle between Townsville and Cooktown, and despite a reputation for cocky confidence, they're easily startled and cautious around humans.

But if the stars align, and you happen to be close when a cassowary breaks from the bush, expect the experience to be exhilarating and perhaps even a little scary. That's not an emotion normally associated with birding, but a cassowary's powerful, claw-tipped feet can disembowel a person with a well-aimed kick.

Bird or dinosaur?
Should you come face-to-face with a cassowary on a jungle trail, half your mind will struggle to make sense of the Edward Lear combination of fluffed-up emu body, sapphire-blue peacock neck and blood-red turkey wattles. The other half will be musing the official safety advice for encounters with a bird that can take down an adult human.

Nine times out of 10, the cassowary will look you up and

Right: The cassowary's headpiece is made from keratin

Below: Cassowaries are most likely seen in rainforest but can sometimes be seen in suburban environments or on beaches

Q&A

Cassowaries have a fierce reputation but what are they really like?
Without any human interaction, the cassowary is a very calm ratite [flightless bird]. It spends its days foraging and roosts wherever it finds itself in the rainforest at dusk. The secret to seeing one is to spend more than a day in the region – they are an endangered species!

Are there any cassowary safety tips?
All cassowaries want to do is forage, so make sure you give them plenty of space. Male cassowaries with chicks often get agitated if people go too close to their chicks.

Any more showstopper birds here?
Summer brings migratory birds from Papua New Guinea, such as metallic starlings and Torresian pied imperial pigeons. All year round we have stunning wompoo fruit doves, noisy pittas, Victoria's riflebirds and double-eyed fig parrots.

Abi Ralph, Daintree Discovery Centre manager

© Martin Pelanek / Shutterstock; Tristan Brown / Getty Images; Imogen Warren / Shutterstock

down with velociraptor intensity, working out the level of threat and the likelihood that you're carrying something tasty to eat. It's quite a withering experience to be sized up by a distant cousin of the long-extinct moa and elephant bird.

More self-assured birds may approach for a closer peek and a few noncommittal feints before disappearing into the undergrowth. But if a cassowary decides to properly charge, hold up a bag or some other bulky object for protection and back away deferentially, staying on your feet – that's not something you have to worry about when spotting sandpipers on the foreshore!

Cassowary hangouts
Beachside picnic spots are some of the best places to try for a cassowary encounter. Around Etty Bay, Mission Beach, Barron Gorge National Park and Cape Tribulation in the Daintree

Right: The wild rainforests and tropical beaches of Cape Tribulation

Far right: An emu on Wilson's Promontory; they're usually seen in groups

Rainforest, cassowaries dwell within dancing distance of backpacker hostels, sometimes strolling out onto the sand or wandering nonchalantly through parking areas and campgrounds.

But you need to be persistent. Try early in the morning, or late in the afternoon in spaces that people have recently departed such as picnic areas and clearings on forest trails – you might just have the birding experience of your life. And even if you don't, the hold-your-breath moment every time you hear a rustle in the undergrowth is a buzz all by itself.

Don't Miss

➡ **Looking a modern-day dinosaur descendant in the eye**

➡ **The thrill of the chase as you comb jungle trails for cassowaries**

➡ **Once-in-a-lifetime photo opportunities, though you'll need to be quick!**

Find Your Joy

Getting there
International flights can whisk you to Cairns, an easy bus ride or drive from Cape Tribulation, Barron Gorge National Park, Mission Beach or Etty Bay. You'll need a 4WD to tackle the Bloomfield Track towards Cooktown.

Accessibility
You don't have to hike to find cassowaries – try your luck on Cape Tribulation beaches and roads around Mission Beach (including the routes to El Arish and Tully).

When to go
Far North Queensland is drenched by rain from December to March, but this is also a good time for cassowary sightings. Be cautious during the breeding and hatching season (June to October); male cassowaries handle the childcare and can be aggressive.

Further information
• No admission charges for most areas.
• Year-round.
• No specialist facilities.
• Restaurants and accommodation in Mission Beach, Etty Bay and Cape Tribulation.
• www. tropicalnorthqueens land.org.au

© Ewen Bell / Lonely Planet; Oscar Cuomo / Shutterstock

Other Australian Big-Bird Locations

Emus, Wilson's Promontory

The emu's reputation for high jinks is mostly invention – they're more skittish than brazen, but they're not hard to spot at lovely Wilson's Prom in Victoria, easily reached from Melbourne. Look for these long-legged lovelies close to areas of cover while walking around the reserve's wildlife-viewing area – you'll be amazed how big they are in the flesh!

Don't miss

Seeing emus on the run – they can reach speeds of 31mph (50km/h), so keep your camera at the ready!

Brolgas, Kakadu National Park

Big critters abound in the Northern Territory, from car-length crocs to Zodiac-sized sharks, but for birders, the brolga is the star of the show. This graceful crane is Australia's biggest wetland bird, and its theatrical, dance-like display during the summer breeding season at Kakadu is guaranteed to raise a smile.

Don't miss

Driving the remote tracks around West Alligator Head to see brolgas cruising over the marshes.

Feel blessed by the sight of lucky white herons

 Tranquil nature, rare birdlife, fern-floored forests

 Mid-September to mid-February

NEW ZEALAND

As you peer out of the hide and across the Waitangiroto River, a flash of snow-white feathers catches your eye. Perched on the branches of a kāmahi tree is a white heron, or kōtuku. It's a picture of elegance with its long neck and pearly feathers, and as the bird takes flight, it looks almost angelic.

Serendipitous sightings

An expression in the Māori language captures this enigmatic sight: 'he kōtuku rerenga tahi' (a white heron's flight is seen but once). But though there are fewer than 200 white herons in all of New Zealand, you don't need luck to see one in Whataroa, on the west coast of New Zealand's South Island. Encounters with these remarkable birds are practically guaranteed at the one-of-a-kind nesting site within Waitangiroto Nature Reserve.

Naturalists believe that New Zealand's original heron population was wind-blown across the Tasman Sea. Ever since, white herons have been creatures of habit: they don't feather their nests anywhere except in the verdant seclusion of Waitangiroto.

Safeguarding white herons

Māori people have long known of this singular nesting site, and the association between white herons and good fortune runs deep. In Māori culture, white herons evoke sacred and singular events, such as the arrival of Kupe, the Polynesian adventurer who discovered the islands we now call New Zealand aboard his mighty ocean-going canoe (waka).

The first European to observe the kōtuku was surveyor Gerhard

Right: Spot birds from Hokitika's treetop walkway

Below: An ethereal kōtuku hunts on the South Island's Waitangiroto River

© Janice Chen / Shutterstock; Lakeview Images / Shutterstock; JerryNZ / Shutterstock

Q&A

Do any heron sightings stand out?
These birds are used to our viewing hide, and they'll land in the trees right in front of our shutters. When this happens, and they're looking at us just 3ft (1m) away, it's really something.

What about non-heron highlights?
Tūī, fantails, bellbirds, wood pigeon and grey warblers are all around. We have lots of coastal areas where you can go and quietly watch small waders like banded dotterels, oystercatchers and pied stilts.

Any restrictions out there?
Be respectful of any signage. There's a big drive to reduce introduced pests, especially stoats and rats. Community groups and the Department of Conservation run predator-control and monitoring programmes.

Where should I head next? Hokitika has a wonderful treetop walkway. South of the glacier country nearing Haast, there are penguins at Lake Moeraki and Monro Beach.

Dion Arnold, White Heron Sanctuary Tours owner

Left: Follow the Kahikatea Swamp Forest Walk in Mt Aspiring National Park

Right: The South Island's charismatic takahē

Don't Miss

→ Admiring orchids and massive ferns in the Kahikatea forest

→ The sight of herons' lacy ornamental breeding plumage

→ Venturing northwest to Ōkārito to look for elusive local kiwis

Mueller, who paddled here in 1865 and wrote of the birds' 'continual "plappering"'– an apt description of their throaty gurgles and cackles. The area wasn't gazetted as a nature reserve until 1957; some 30 years later, the local Arnold family began tours to the nesting site, building a hide to ensure minimal disturbance of these precious birds.

Teeming wetlands

When you join a tour, a minivan trundles through farmland and deep into the reserve, a patchwork of marshland and white pine forests that fringe the Waitangiroto River. After a short walk through the rainforests of Kahikatea, where some trees are more than a millennium old, you reach a hide where you can observe these elegant birds.

Although white herons are the stars of the show, you can also spot royal spoonbills swaggering through the wetlands and digging in the shallows with their bulbous-ended beaks, as well as little shags preening on low-hanging boughs.

White herons at rest might appear squat and unremarkable. Like pale goblins, they hunch over squawking chicks, which have punk-rock down feathers protruding from their little bodies. But then you see an adult bird extend its long, S-shaped neck, like a ballerina striking a pose. Its veil of iridescent plumage catches the light – a flash of beauty that cuts through the shadows. In this lush green corner of Whataroa, good luck can be found in unexpected places.

Find Your Joy

Getting there
Infrequent seasonal InterCity buses link Whataroa and Franz Josef (19 miles/31km away), but most people drive. Note that some people refer to Whataroa's nesting site as the 'Ōkārito colony' – Ōkārito is actually west of Whataroa, though white herons feed in Ōkārito Lagoon.

Accessibility
Transport is by minivan followed by a level 2625ft-long (800m) walking trail. Though it isn't fully wheelchair-accessible, the tour is suitable for most ability levels, with assistance available for those with limited mobility.

When to go
Mid-September to mid-February for dozens of white herons guarding hungry chicks; but there are year-round rainforest tours to spot ferns, orchids and native birds.

Further information
• Admission charge; reserve ahead.
• Mid-September to mid-February.
• Hides available.
• Fill up at the Lonely Stag, oppositethe tour departure point.
• Accommodation in Whataroa, Franz Josef and Harihari.
• www.whiteherontours. co.nz

© Karel Stipek / Shutterstock; VMJones / Getty Images

Other South Island Rare Birds

Takahē, Te Anau Bird Sanctuary

Somewhere between a royal blue turkey and a prehistoric lizard is the takahē. These flightless birds with powerful beaks and mighty red claws were believed extinct until their rediscovery in 1948. Today, takahē encounters are guaranteed at Te Anau Bird Sanctuary, part of a network of breed-and-release sanctuaries growing the population of these remarkable groundbirds.

Don't miss

Admiring other colourful residents like the plump kererū (wood pigeon) and endangered kākā (parrot).

Orange-fronted parakeets, Marlborough Sounds

Bright green with a patch of orange and yellow above its curved beak, the kākāriki karaka is New Zealand's rarest parakeet. There are fewer than 450 birds in the wild, but your best chance of spotting this neon-hued beauty is at the northern end of the South Island, on predator-free Blumine Island (Ōruawairua). Take a water taxi from Picton and bring your best binoculars.

Don't miss

Spotting another rare species, the black-and-white king shag, with its distinctive rose-pink feet.

Caper in the company of cockatoos in Far North Queensland

♡ Wild nature, rare encounters, sensory overload

🕐 June to October

AUSTRALIA

If you really want to get away from it all, you could do worse than Cape York. Some of the dirt roads that snake up to Australia's northernmost tip see just a few dozen vehicles a year – but you'll never be alone. Wildlife fills the void, from fearsome salties (saltwater crocodiles) to birdlife to make ornithologists feel giddy as schoolkids.

Spend the night in one of the bush campgrounds north of Laura and your mornings will be kickstarted not by the crowing of roosters but by a mixed cacophony of birdsong, from the chunter of parrots and the music-hall cackle of kookaburras to the school-bus-getting-out-of-hand shrieks of visiting cockatoos.

Wildlife-filled emptiness
Part of the thrill of exploring this blissfully empty peninsula – home to just 0.04 people per square kilometre, on a par with the Gobi Desert – is escaping into untamed nature. And nature will come to you, both inside and outside the Cape's rugged national parks.

That might mean striped possums snuffling through your campsite while you sleep, or Jack Russell–sized fruit bats swooping overhead at sunset. Or it could mean 50-odd cockatoos, filling every tree and waking you from your slumbers with an almost human babble of conversation.

Cockatoos are easily spotted in this rugged corner of Australia, known locally as the Tip (Pajinka, to Aboriginal Australians) – with the notable exception of the rare palm cockatoo (*Probosciger aterrimus*), an elusive, rouge-cheeked rock star who hides out in remote parts of the peninsula.

Right: A sulphur-crested cocktoo picks seeds from a yellow bottle-brush tree

Below: Gangs of cockatoos tend to have one dominant male and female pair

My Birding Joy

It's quite a shock to wake up somewhere you expect to be alone and find the air full of noise. While four-wheel-driving through Cape York, I parked up by a billabong and went to sleep on the back seat, feeling reasonably confident that there wasn't another living soul for miles. My mistake – at dawn, I was rudely awakened by what sounded like rioting fans at a football match.

Wiping the mist from the windows in a state of alarm, I saw dozens of sulphur-crested cockatoos in the trees around my impromptu campsite, screeching and blustering like the home team had just won the cup. As I opened the door, they took flight, filling the sky with white feathers and noise, before vanishing over the treetops, leaving me once again alone in the silence – it was certainly one of my more memorable wake-up calls!

Joe Bindloss

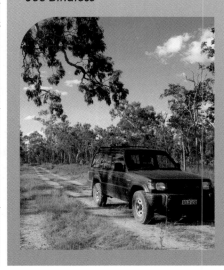

© John Carnemolla / Shutterstock; Frank Fichtmueller / Shutterstock; Suzanne Long / Alamy Stock Photo

But that doesn't diminish the spectacle when a chattering – the common noun for cockatoos – comes to call.

One moment, the skies will be silent. The next, the air will be alive with flapping wings and babbling bills. Sulphur-crested cockatoos and parrot cousins such as little corellas move in large congregations, marking their arrival with an explosion of noise. In the quiet of the Outback, it's a reminder that the bush is as alive as any city, with cockatoos as the self-appointed town criers.

Seeing these magnificent birds at play will also remind you that the wildlife is fully at home in this unforgiving environment, while you are just a poorly adapted passer-by. With a strong nose for water and nutcracker beaks evolved for busting open jungle seeds, cockatoos will find sustenance in this arid landscape while you're desperately waiting for the

Right: A formidable palm cockatoo on Queensland's Cape York

Far right: Red crabs migrate across Christmas Island annually, causing a feeding frenzy for birds

rescue party to arrive.

Above all though, watching cockatoos is a celebration of life. Their movements, their remarkable dexterity (cockatoos are zygodactyl, gripping objects precisely with two forward-facing and two backward-facing toes), the way they puff up their crests like politicians about to launch into a blistering oratory, and of course their raucous calls, are the embodiment of avian joie de vivre. It'll leave you smiling long after the last screeches have faded into the distance.

Don't Miss

→ **Bedding down at a bush campground, surrounded by wildlife**

→ **The sky suddenly filling with noise as a chattering of cockatoos swoops in**

→ **Encounters with palm cockatoos – if you're very lucky!**

Find Your Joy

Getting there
The push to the Tip is a famous test of off-road endurance. To safely navigate the Old Telegraph Track – the most popular and dramatic route – you'll need a well-equipped 4WD, food and water, and a means of making contact in emergencies. Book national park campsites in advance (https://parks.des.qld.gov.au/camping/bookings).

Accessibility
If you can drive or be driven, birding in Cape York is definitely within reach, but most accommodation is at basic campsites with limited facilities.

When to go
June to October is the optimum driving window. The weather is dry, road surfaces harden and water levels drop, making it easier to ford creeks and rivers on the way to the Tip.

Further information
• Free to visitors.
• Year-round, but tricky in the rainy season.
• No specialist facilities.
• This is camping country, but a few scattered roadhouse pubs serve meals.

© Kensho Photographic / Shutterstock; Genevieve Vallee / Alamy Stock Photo

Other Wild Australian Birding Sites

Christmas Island, Western Australia

Named by a British East India Company captain who sailed by on Christmas Day 1643, this outpost isle is famed for its astonishing red crab migration (October–December), but it's also a stunning birding spot, home to species that never learned to fear humans in the absence of native predators. Top spots include goshawks, boobies, golden bosun birds (white-tailed tropicbirds) and Christmas Island imperial pigeons.

Don't miss
Encounters with Christmas Island frigatebirds, with their distinctive crab-red neck pouches.

Gluepot Reserve, South Australia

Once a remote sheep station, this wild patch of mallee scrub and bushland inland from Adelaide is a birders' playground, and a slice of real Australian Outback. BirdLife Australia volunteers are on hand to help you track down such characters as black-eared miners, owlet-nightjars and chestnut quail-thrushes.

Don't miss
Seeking sightings of 18 threatened Australian bird species – including scarlet-chested parrots and striated grasswrens – with an expert local guide.

Index

The Joy of Birdwatching

August 2024

Published by Lonely Planet Global Limited

CRN 554153

www.lonelyplanet.com

1 2 3 4 5 6 7 8 9 10

Printed in Malaysia

ISBN 978 18375 8265 5

© Lonely Planet 2024

© photographers as indicated 2024

Written by Anita Isalska, Anna Richards, Annika S Hipple, Bella Falk, Bradley Mayhew, Brendan Sainsbury, Craig MacLachlan, Elizabeth Lavis, Erik Trinidad, Jennifer Hattam, Jesse Scott, Joanna Cooke, Joe Bindloss, Kate Armstrong, Kerry Walker, Mark Eveleigh, Mary Fitzpatrick, Mike MacEacheran, Dr Mya Rose-Craig, Nicholas DeRenzo, Pat Kinsella, Paul Stafford, Sarah Gilbert, Sarah Kuta, Simon Richmond, SJ Armstrong, Steve Fallon, Stuart Butler, Tenijah Hamilton, Virginia Jealous, Willem Span

Publishing Director: Piers Pickard
Illustrated & Gift Publisher: Becca Hunt
Senior Editor: Robin Barton
Senior Designer: Emily Dubin
Commissioning Editor: Joe Bindloss
Editor: Polly Thomas
Designer: Jo Dovey
Cover and illustration: Owen Gatley
Print Production: Nigel Longuet

All rights reserved.

No part of this publication may be reproduced, stored in a retrieval system or transmitted in any form by any means, electronic, mechanical, photocopying, recording or otherwise except brief extracts for the purpose of review, without the written permission of the publisher. Lonely Planet and the Lonely Planet logo are trademarks of Lonely Planet and are registered in the US patent and Trademark Office and in other countries.

Lonely Planet Global Ltd Office

Digital Depot, Roe Lane (off Thomas St), Digital Hub, Dublin 8, D08 TCV4 Ireland

STAY IN TOUCH

lonelyplanet.com/contact

Although the authors and Lonely Planet have taken all reasonable care in preparing this book, we make no warranty about the accuracy or completeness of its content and, to the maximum extent permitted, disclaim all liability from its use.

Paper in this book is certified against the Forest Stewardship Council™ standards. FSC™ promotes environmentally responsible, socially beneficial and economically viable management of the world's forests.